Greg Norman

ADVANCED GOLF

Photography by Leonard Kamsler

Foreword by Raymond Floyd

Paperback edition published in the United States in 1996 by Journey Editions, an imprint of Charles E. Tuttle Co., Inc., of Rutland, Vermont and Tokyo, Japan, with editorial offices at 153 Milk Street, Boston, Massachusetts 02109.

First published in the United States in 1995 by Charles E. Tuttle Co., Inc.

ISBN 1-885203-34-9

Cataloging-in-Publication Data is available for this title from the Library of Congress.

Produced by Roeder Publications Pte. Ltd.
Printed by CS Graphics Pte. Ltd.

FOREWORD

When a treasured friend and fellow competitor on the PGA TOUR asked me to introduce his new instructional book, I was tremendously honored. Greg Norman is known and admired by everyone who follows golf as the magnificent player from Down Under. Called the "Shark" for his distinctive and aggressive style of play, he very well may be the greatest golfer in the world today.

Even with his enormous talent, Greg also has a burning desire to improve. That ambition to improve upon established excellence obviously identified a devoted student of golf. Greg learned to play golf by observing good players, avidly reading instructional material and, of course, by constant practice. He has demonstrated a thorough understanding of all aspects of the game, a good eye for the mechanics of the swing and an effective way of communicating his vast knowledge.

Only a fortunate few know Greg Norman, the person, a caring and thoughtful athlete who gives so much back to the game and its charitable causes. Generous with his time and wisdom, he has frequently aided fellow players with their games.

Earlier this year, I was in a terrible putting slump. Greg spotted a couple of flaws in my stroke while we were playing a practice round at the PGA Championship at Southern Hills. With his suggestions I immediately started putting like the old Ray Floyd again. Not many touring pros would take the time to help a competitor during the course of a major championship, but that was typical of Greg Norman. He wants to beat you when you're playing your best game.

In this book he shares with readers many of his unique insights on the game and how it is played and enjoyed. Greg is the best overall driver of ball that I have ever seen, and the rest of his game isn't far behind. Against the scenic backdrop of his new course, the Medalist Club, in Hobe Sound, Florida, Greg Norman has revealed many of the secrets of his success in graphics and very readable narrative.

I am sure that you will enjoy this book and add it to your own golf library as a remarkable reference whenever you feel the need to sharpen your game.

Raymond Floyd

Raymond Floyd

CONTENTS

CONTENTS

CONTENTS

CONTENTS

INTRODUCTION

The world of golf has been significantly different since the arrival of Greg Norman. The Great White Shark is without doubt one of the most watched golfers on the planet and has been since he won his first tournament in Australia in 1977. Since then, he has achieved more than 70 victories worldwide, including the 1986 and 1993 British Open Championships.

Greg has always been an exceptional talent because of the rare combination of his great athleticism, sheer aggressiveness on the course and all-round skill. Simply, he can play golf at a level higher than not just amateur golfers but the vast majority of touring professionals.

He excites fans, intimidates rivals and entertains in a way that inspires. His emergence on the international scene was not so much a knocking politely and asking to come in but rather a slapping back of the bat-wing doors as if he were a gunslinger walking into a Wild West saloon. Americans awakened when the Shark produced a brilliant charge in his first Masters Tournament in 1981, finishing fourth, and ever since they have had a love affair with Australia's finest golfer. Of course, Greg's countrymen were already on the bandwagon and Europe had experienced a few Norman conquests. Dan Jenkins of Golf Digest said he looked like the club pro from Mount Olympus.

Greg is continually reminding us of how brilliant a golfer he is with some of the most memorable performances in the history of the game. Who will forget his closing 64 to overtake Nick Faldo in the 1993 British Open at Royal St. George's, his closing round of 62 and eagle on the first playoff hole of Doral's Blue Monster in 1992, his 63 enroute to winning the 1986 British Open at Turnberry?

Greg's game is based on power, but he has the great ability to harness it, play the explosive shot when required or finesse the ball with the touch of a surgeon. A major reason for this is his great experience as a world golfer, at first honing his skills on the hard, fast and difficult seaboard courses of Australia, then battling and conquering the elements in Europe, and eventually entering the cauldron of the United States PGA.

I have always been a fan of Greg Norman. I had watched him closely from a distance long before I became his coach in 1990. At that stage, he was a disappointed man. Several Majors that should have been his by right had painfully eluded him. He had lost his play-off in the 1984 US Open to Fuzzy Zoeller. And in 1986 – the year he won the British Open for the first time – he lost the Masters by one stroke to Jack Nicklaus and the PGA to Bob Tway.

By then, I knew his swing by heart, I had analyzed it thoroughly and knew exactly what was wrong with it. I was ready to rebuild his swing before he even asked. When he did, it changed my life.

There is no doubt in my mind that Greg is the most talented golfer I will ever coach. I believe that there is no tournament he cannot win and no shot he cannot play. But he is also by far the most fascinating personality I have ever met.

He is one person who will always speak his mind. And he has no qualms about showing his emotions either. He can stare you down with unforgiving eyes you will not easily forget or flash his million-dollar smile and set the gallery on fire. He enjoys the gallery; he enjoys sharing his game, his feelings with them. I remember how he walked to the first tee box on the first day of the 1993 Australian Masters, with tears streaming down his face when he learned that the son of a friend had died.

Greg has always been adventurous. When he was a 17-year-old lad in Queensland, Australia, his dream was to become a fighter pilot. He thrives on a good challenge and stiff competition. He is determined to win every time he tees off. But it doesn't stop at golf. He wants to be the best at everything he does.

Even as a kid, Greg was athletic. He excelled in diving, played rugby, cricket, squash and Australian football. When he picked up his mother's golf clubs for the first time, aged 15, he managed to smash a ball 330 yards without problems. He went on to win the fourth professional tournament he entered at 21 against the competition of Peter Thomson, Bruce Devlin and David Graham. He took Japan and Europe by storm, and by the time he entered the US circuit in 1981, the Great White Shark was born.

In the meantime, he has worked tirelessly on his game and rounded it from one of raw aggression to that of the consummate competitor who adapts to any condition. He is the most brilliant driver off the tee; with a short game to match.

It is these experiences and skills that he brings to the reader in ADVANCED GOLF. Obviously, he plays golf at a level we can only dream of, but his technique, imagination and execution offer a great insight into how to prepare for and play the game. His wonderful tuition will help you to better your own game.

One of the greatest shotmakers in the history of golf takes us from the tee to the green, demonstrating the way an advanced player thinks about and executes shots, stopping to show how to deal with every eventuality.

ADVANCED GOLF is a book about working your game. Greg shows you the shots to play and explains their execution. He talks about his new, improved swing from driving the ball through to putting. He tells you how to plan your strategy and how to deal with climate and weather conditions, with bad lies in the rough and with disconcerting bunker shots, to build a better score.

Follow Greg's examples, be inspired like the millions of Norman fans before you and learn to use your imagination. You will develop the skills and confidence to take your game to another level.

C l a u d e   (B u t c h)   H a r m o n ,   J r .   *

* The photograph on page 178 shows Butch with Greg.

1. Power

THE SWING

I should like to share with you my repertoire of shotmaking techniques acquired over almost twenty years of professional golf. I have worked - and still work - endlessly on my shots and my swing out of a determination to be the best - at everything I do. Believe me, if you are as serious about improving your score, you will succeed.

Before inviting you to fine-tune your shotmaking skills and sending you off to the driving range, let me reveal to you my secret for a controlled and powerful swing. It will help you to gain both distance and accuracy with your shots.

My father used to tell me that in order to win I had to learn to control myself and the environment around me. To control your mind and body throughout a round of golf with all its pressures and frustrations is probably the single biggest challenge in golf. Since there is little you can do about the divots, the hazards and the humps on the fairways, you have even more reason to get a grip on your mind and your club before teeing off.

I have my bad days like you do. But on my good days, I can hit the ball from 180 yards to within a foot of my target, time after time. I am in perfect control of the club and the ball. I feel that the grip, the club and the ball are part of me. I swing in my own rhythm. The tempo is the key to control over the swing.

You have to swing in harmony with yourself and your equipment if you want to improve. Without finding and maintaining your own rhythm, you will not be able to swing consistently well; and there can be no power and precision in your stroke. To keep your tempo throughout your game, start by simplifying the changes you make for each shot.

No matter what kind of stroke you play or what sort of club you use, you need to make only minute adjustments for shotmaking; to finesse chip shots, for instance, you need to work the hands more; or to shape the line of flight, you may alter the ball position. But for simple, straightforward shots, you should swing in the same manner from the driver all the way down to the nine-iron, like I do.

On my regular shot, I hit every ball off the same spot opposite my left heel. I do not move the ball back towards the middle of my stance - even for the short irons. The only difference you can find in my stance is that I tilt my waist more as the clubs become shorter.

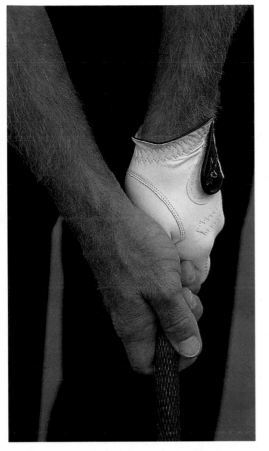

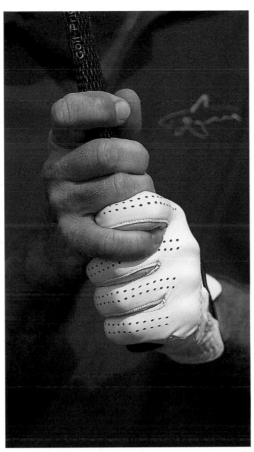

I use a variation of the overlapping grip. Instead of overlapping, however, I just mesh the last finger of my right hand with the forefinger of the left hand.
FAR LEFT: You can see that the V in the left hand and the V in the right hand point towards the right ear. My grip is neither strong nor weak, as the left hand shows two knuckles. LEFT: The fingers are meshed together.
BELOW LEFT: There is no overlapping in my grip.

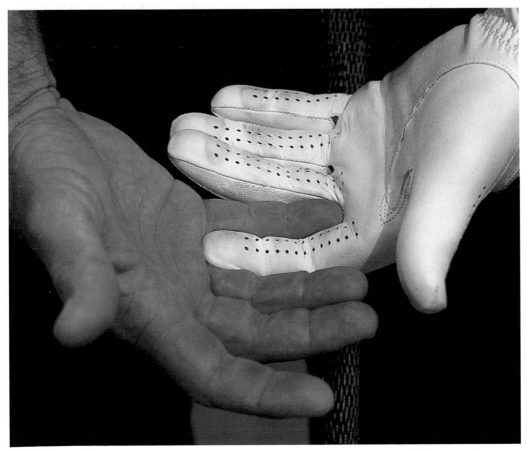

THE STANCE

RIGHT: *As you can see, the ball position stays the same with the driver, the two-iron and the nine-iron. I believe in a constant ball position opposite the left heel, in line with the left armpit. My left foot is pointing approximately 20 degrees to the left. Note that the clubhead is hovering behind the ball, allowing my arms to hang down unobstructed.*
CENTER RIGHT: *The weight is evenly distributed, with 50 percent on each foot.*
FAR RIGHT: *The only difference you can find in my stance is that I tilt my waist more as the clubs become shorter. Following my example will add consistency to your game.*

THE TAKEAWAY

RIGHT, BELOW RIGHT AND BOTTOM RIGHT: *A one-piece takeaway can be achieved with each club by keeping the triangle that is formed by the chest and the arms together as you start the backswing.*

THE BACKSWING

FAR RIGHT AND OPPOSITE: *The shoulder has turned to the right of the target line by about 110 degrees with the driver, almost as far with the long iron and still 90 degrees with the short iron at the top of the backswing. The head has moved slightly to the right following the shoulder behind the ball. Note that the left heel remains on the ground.*

FAR LEFT: *You can combine both power and balance, as can be seen in this follow through with the driver. The shoulders are turned about 110 degrees to the left from their address position with the driver, almost as far with the long iron, and approximately 100 degrees with the nine-iron.* **CENTER LEFT:** *My weight is on my left side and my body has fully rotated around so that my belt buckle is facing the target. There is hardly any difference between the driver and the two-iron.* **LEFT:** *As you can see, my arms and club shaft are all in the same position.*

OPPOSITE, FROM LEFT TO RIGHT, TOP TO BOTTOM: *The weight transfer is crucial to the length and success of all your shots, but probably more so for the driver. The flex of the knees gives you an indication of the weight transfer. The straighter the knee, the more weight it carries. Remember that your weight should always go in the direction the club is swinging. The weight shifts to the inside of the right foot at the start of the backswing. At the top of the swing, about 65 to 70 percent of the weight is concentrated on the right side. The weight moves back to the left side at the start of the downswing. Through the impact zone, you can see that the weight has turned onto the ball of the left foot. When the swing is complete, the weight is totally on the left side.*

The steeper swing plane, imposed by the shorter club shafts, suffices to hit irons correctly without any adjustment of the ball position. I find it easier to maintain my rhythm and timing by repeating exactly the same action over and over with every shot and every club. The repetition triggers the muscle-memory, letting me play consistently well.

The Grip

The grip is the only contact you have with the club. It controls the clubhead throughout your swing and determines the success of your shot. If your grip is faulty, you need to counteract your mistake through adjustments in your swing if you hope to square the club face at impact.

When I started out in golf observing and copying players on the course near my home, I tried the Vardon, the baseball, and other grips. However, I needed a grip that involved my fingers more than these did in order to be able to work and finesse the ball as much or as little as I needed to. Of course, such adjustments are so minute that if they could be measured at all, we'd be talking millimeters. To be able to gauge the adjustments correctly, I needed a more precise feel of how the club was reacting to them than I got from my hands in any of the standard grips.

In the end, I adopted a variation of the overlapping grip. The only difference from the basic version of the grip is that I don't lay the small finger of my right hand across the forefinger of the left hand; instead, the right small finger rests snugly in the depression between the left forefinger and middle finger.

The position of my grip on the club balances the strength evenly between the left and the right hand. You can see in the photographs on page 17 that two knuckles are showing on the left hand. A weak grip would show one and a half knuckles, while a strong one would show two and a half.

I found no benefit in either a strong or a weak grip, although a strong grip can cure a slice by allowing the right hand to roll over fast at impact, closing the club face. Conversely, a weak grip can offset a hook since it is harder to close the club face at impact. Did you over-compensate for your beginner's mistakes long ago? If you are afflicted with a sideways curvature that you don't intend in your shots, change your grip to a neutral position.

A neutral grip ensures that both hands release together at impact and strike the ball powerfully. The closer the hands are together, the better they work as one, adding precision and consistency to your game. A neutral grip may reward you with wonderfully straight, and, consequently, long shots.

*My pre-shot routine helps me
to play consistently well.
PREVIOUS PAGES FROM
LEFT TO RIGHT, TOP TO
BOTTOM: I have a very
precise pre-shot routine
which I repeat before each
and every shot I hit. I start
from behind the ball where I
visualize the shot I want to
play. I hold the club in two
hands, while I feel its
weight. I imagine the
intended trajectory of my
shot and select the highest
point the ball will reach in
its flight as my immediate
target. I aim my shot
directly at this point in the
sky and let the gravity carry
the ball to its ultimate
destination. Try this
technique. It will help you to
hit powerful drives. I then
ground the club on my target
line, step in with my left foot
and set the width of my
stance with my right foot. I
look up from the ball to the
point in the air I have
chosen, and then to my
target. When I focus again
on the ball, I do two waggles
and am ready for my shot. A
pre-shot routine is essential
for a consistent game.*

Grip pressure is a widely overlooked aspect of your only connection with the club. It is also a very personal affair. Sam Snead asks you to hold the grip as if it was a bird in your hand. John Daly talks about holding it like a loaf of bread.

Regardless of the image you want to use to describe your grip pressure, it must not be too tight or else it causes tension in your hands and arms, which makes it difficult for you to get the feel for the shot. A grip that is too tight will also prevent you from releasing naturally at impact. On the other hand, if you grip the club too lightly, you lose control over the clubhead on your backswing. As a result, you may not be able to square the club face to the target at impact.

Keep your grip pressure steady throughout your swing on all your shots - with very few exceptions - and you will find it easier to keep your tempo.

The Pre-Shot Routine

To consistently maintain timing and rhythm in your golf swing, you must never deviate from your pre-shot routine. This should be quite obvious, but I have watched good golfers in pro-ams changing their routine from one shot to another, with predictably bad results. And I have been guilty of the offense as well.

I have to say it again: you must never deviate from your pre-shot routine. This holds true regardless of the name of the game, be it a practice session, a friendly match or an important tournament. A pre-shot routine is as individual as your fingerprints. I will tell you and show you exactly what I do, to impress upon you the importance of the slightest little detail in a set routine. (I wonder if you could tell me offhand how many times you waggle.)

When I have selected the club, I walk up to the ball in line with the target as I plan my strategy. I take the bearings of the fairway ahead, scout the hazards, and visualize the length and line of the shot I want to hit. I set the club face on the target line, with my right foot very nearly in its address position parallel to the target and my left foot at an angle to the right foot, pointing at the target.

Then, I step in with my left foot and back with my right to find the right width of my stance for this shot. When I have adjusted the stance, I bend down for the address; and from that position, I take another look at the target line, with the clubhead hovering behind the ball. Before I start on the takeaway, I waggle twice to feel the weight of the club and to relax the tension in my wrist.

The Stance

The width of the stance is really the foundation of a good swing. When Butch Harmon started to coach me, one of the first things he did was to check my set-up position from behind. At address, your right shoulder, your right knee, and the ball of your right foot must form a straight line. Ask your coach or playing partner to check your stance for you. Your posture may be different from what you thought it was. And poor posture will lead to a poor takeaway.

At address, the inside of your feet should be approximately shoulder-width apart. A wider stance reduces the hip turn, which allows you to tighten the backswing. You can control your swing better this way. However, if you are standing with your feet too far apart, your knees cannot flex very much and your hips can hardly rotate at all. Your shoulder turn will be very much reduced, and you will lose considerable distance on your shots.

If your stance is too narrow, your swing is not based on a solid footing and a body rotation will throw you off balance. Believe me, I know what I am talking about. I used to have a very narrow stance and quite often ended up with the weight not on, but outside my right leg at the top of my backswing. In other words: I was sliding, and my lower body would not rotate. On the downswing, all I could do was cast from the top, instead of swinging through smoothly with my right hand.

Despite countless tournaments and endless days of hitting balls on the driving range, my swing had deteriorated to such a point that I needed professional help just to get back to basics. If this could happen to me, it certainly can happen to you.

Check your hip position - both at the backswing and the follow through - if you have doubts about your body rotation. Your hips should turn about 35 degrees away from your address alignment; not more because the tension in the body works like a spring. The higher the tension between hips and shoulders, the greater the clubhead speed you will generate. If you flex your knees well and your hips still can't rotate that far, your stance is probably too wide. If you start swaying, it is too narrow.

I ground the club squarely facing the target and place my left foot opposite the clubhead, with the tip of the left foot pointing by about 20 degrees to the left. This foot position is crucial for the power of your game. It ensures that you can quickly move the left side of your body out of the way of the clubhead near impact, meaning you can accelerate more through impact and gain distance on your shot.

I then adjust the right foot in line with the left foot and the clubhead, perpendicular to the target line. This helps to anchor your swing and to prevent you from shifting sideways. This position also limits your hip turn and prevents knee dipping and a false backswing. Don't forget to align your shoulders parallel to your feet as well, if you want to square the club face at impact.

The ball position on most of my swings is off the left heel, with the ball in line with my the left armpit. Retaining a constant ball position whenever possible allows me to hit most of my shots in exactly the same way, with as few adjustments to my swing as possible. It is just common sense when you think about it. The less you change your swing, the more consistent your game.

For maximum distance, tilt your waist and flex your knees until you are comfortable throughout your swing. When taking your stance, think of trying to tilt a bar stool you are sitting on. If you stand too tall, you will curtail your body turn. If you bend too much, you will hit the ball with the heel.

I hold my club - with its sweet spot right behind the ball - slightly off the ground at address to relieve any tension in my arms and to keep a constant pressure on my grip. I also find it easier to concentrate on the shot if my arms and club hang down without any obstruction. This address position virtually guarantees that the swing action will start in one piece.

Let your arms drop down naturally to grip your club. If you have to stretch to reach the ball with the clubhead, you are standing too far from the ball. During the swing, tensions will build in your upper body and your shoulder turn will be obstructed. If you stand too close, you will be forced to stand taller again and lose distance as well.

At address, your weight should be evenly distributed between your legs for the clubs you use, with the exception of the wedges. You will then have a comfortable and solid base to hit forcefully at the ball.

The Takeaway

A perfect swing should look like it is cast in one piece. Every muscle, every joint and the club itself must all move together. I do not consciously start the takeaway by taking any isolated action. I would feel totally uncoordinated if I did. Looking at the photographs on page 20, you will immediately recognize the triangle formed by my chest and arms at address. When I initiate the takeaway, this triangle stays intact. All the movements integrated into the beginning of the swing start together.

To set up for a wide swing arc, begin the takeaway low and slow by jointly turning your hands, arms, and shoulders away from the ball and shifting your weight to your right foot. A good check-point for you is when your wrists start to cock (vertically) and the club has traveled to the height of your waist. The club shaft must then be in line with your feet, with the toe of your club pointed up, and your arms extended parallel to the target line as far to the right as they can go. Keep your right arm on top of your left.

You are now set up to create the kind of shoulder and hip turn that guarantees maximum distance for your shot. The wider the swing arc, the more clubhead speed you generate, and, subsequently, the further the ball flies.

The Backswing

As your shoulders start to turn, your weight is transferred to the inside of the right foot since your weight follows the direction the clubhead takes. The remaining weight on your left leg will shift towards its right side as well. At this point, stop your weight from moving past the center of your right foot so that you don't end up shifting instead of turning, as I used to do.

It is very easy from this position to lift the left heel. Your body rotation may pull it up as you turn. As a matter of fact, the less flexible you are, the higher your heel tends to be pulled up. Resist it. Do stretching exercises to become more supple if you must. A firmly grounded left heel lends stability to your swing; a lifted heel can affect your swing plane.

The flex of your right knee should not change at all, with both your knees rotating until the left points to the right of the ball. This, again, will help you to turn further and unleash more power at impact.

Keep the triangle formed by your arms and chest together as long as you can. A deviating elbow or a collapsing wrist will lead you to leave your swing plane. It is quite astonishing how many players are able to counteract their swing mistakes through impact, but their loss in distance and accuracy cannot be offset. To hit a ball perfectly, you need a perfectly controlled swing.

My wrists carry the club until it is perpendicular to my right shoulder. Since the neck is attached to the shoulders, the head must move back ever so slightly as you make your turn. At the top of my swing, my back is facing the target, my left shoulder is well behind the ball almost to the point where it is aligned to the inside of my right knee, and my head has moved behind the ball. I have extended the left arm and don't allow my hands to drop behind the head, but rather arch out away from my head at the top of the swing.

My elbow points down and a little behind me, indicating that my shoulders have turned 110 degrees to the right, while the hips should not rotate further than 35 degrees to maintain the tension of the body coil for a powerful release. You may not be able to emulate exactly the length of my body turn but if you stretch to the maximum of your capability, the length of your shots will increase, take my word for it.

An ideal test for the correct club position at the top of the swing is to let go of the club. It should come to rest on the right shoulder - or at the very least touch it. If the swing is too flat, the club will drop behind you. If your club crossed the target line, it would drop on your head.

A wide swing arc and a tremendous shoulder turn are the main components for a powerful swing. But do stop in time. If you allow the clubhead to drop past parallel to the ground, gravity will pull it down further, prompting you to cock your wrists more. When you then start your downswing, you will not only have to straighten out your wrists again but you will also have to bring the club back to parallel. You would be better off saving yourself the trouble, and instead spending the energy and effort to increase your clubhead speed.

The Downswing

The downswing is the fastest and most crucial part of the swing, since it leads you to deliver the clubhead to the ball. Put the downswing on a proper footing, literally, by starting it from the ground up, through a weight transfer from the right to the left foot, with a slight lateral leg drive.

The left knee and left hip rotate to the left to allow shoulder, hands and arms to follow the lead of the legs while staying close to the body. The centrifugal force of the swing carries your arms and hands through impact as your right shoulder comes under the chin. The back of your left hand should be squared to the target. Extend your arms fully to the left side and let your right arm cross over the left after impact.

I see many golfers on their right toes at impact. This not only puts them on a very shaky foundation for a solid ball contact but also disrupts the tension in the muscles necessary for maximum clubhead speed. It is important for you to maintain the foot position that you had at address through impact, as I do. In other words: keep your feet flat on the ground until after impact.

The distance of your shot is proportional to the clubhead speed you apply through impact. To increase your release momentum, your hips should be turned about 35 degrees to the left at impact and your chest 15 degrees. This position ensures that your arms and hands now have ample space to power through impact, preventing you from trying to hit the ball with the upper body. Keep your head behind the movement to ensure that the club face is squared through impact, not only at impact. The line of flight is shaped as the ball leaves the club face, not as it is struck initially.

The Follow Through

After impact, the momentum of your swing carries the club naturally to the follow through, which extends longer but lower than the backswing. The follow through winds around the body to the left until the hands reach shoulder height, without carrying the club above the shoulders as they did on the backswing.

As you turn squarely to the target, your hips are still slightly tilted to the right. The head has remained somewhat behind the movement for better balance. My belt buckle points to the target, and my shoulders have turned 110 degrees to the left from the address position.

Viewed from behind, the club shaft should point right across your neck in continuation of the swing arc, resulting in a follow through that is longer than the backswing. The right shoulder tries to follow behind the ball. There is hardly any weight left on the right foot, and the left leg is flexed very little and almost upright. If your left leg is still bent, you may have slid sideways.

A follow through cannot be faked; it can only be as good as your swing was. It is as significant for a powerful stroke as your backswing, because the width of your swing arc determines the clubhead speed. An incomplete finish means that you decelerated through impact or deviated from your swing plane. Either fault will have cost you distance and accuracy.

2. Equipment

THE DRIVER

OVERLEAF, PAGE 34: *To maximize distance and precision in your drive, set up in perfect posture. The inside of your feet should be as far apart as the width of your shoulders. The ball is positioned opposite the left armpit, with your arms hanging straight down from your shoulders.* PAGE 38 and 39: *Take the club away low and slow, maintaining the triangle formed by your shoulders and arms.* PAGES 40 AND 41: *A very wide arc and a full shoulder turn help set the club in a perfect position.* PAGES 42 AND 43: *At the top of the swing, you have turned your left shoulder behind the ball and the weight has shifted to the inside of your right foot. The shoulders have turned approximately 110 degrees, while the hips have rotated 60 degrees. Try to turn as far as you can for your most powerful drive.* PAGES 44 AND 45: *The downswing starts from the ground up. The weight transfers back to the left side, allowing the arms and hands to drop down naturally into a position to be delivered to the ball squarely. The left knee and left hip rotate to the left to prevent my lower body from obstructing my arms through impact.* PAGES 46 AND 47: *At impact, my hip has rotated 35 degrees to the left from the address position and my*

M uch of the success of your drives is determined by the distance of your hit. Most of the total score of your round is, in turn, decided by the success of your drives. Why? The reason is that a mishit drive cannot be made good. A golfer's overall performance usually suffers in consequence, since his confidence is shaken. If you duff your drive on a par five, it will cost at least one additional stroke. If you duff your drive on a par four of medium length, you need to place a mid iron on the green, probably hitting out of the rough. Are you confident that you can get it close to the hole? A strong, straight drive would leave you on the same hole with a short iron approach instead. Which would you prefer?

A powerful drive is composed of confidence, rhythm, and a wide swing arc - in that order. It has nothing to do with muscular strength or a rapid swing. And any single component will not let you achieve your goal either; they must work together in your swing. Let me show you how to put more power into your drives without spraying the balls all over the fairways.

My drives are usually powerful, long and straight but if need be I can shape them just as easily to the left or right. There are players who drive either for length or for position, but not I. All my drives are positioned and I can reduce their length at will. I am so confident and comfortable with the driver in my hand that I don't hesitate to use it even if I could opt for an iron on crucial holes in major tournaments.

After Butch reworked my swing, one of my first big tests was the 1993 British Open Championship at Royal St. George's. It was my driving that set the solid foundation for my attack on the course, and I built on it during the final round. I held a one-stroke lead when my playing partner, Bernhard Langer, hit his tee shot out-of-bounds on the 14th hole. Conventional wisdom would have had me use an iron off the tee to nurse the lead on that par five, but this thought did not cross my mind for a second.

Apart from Langer, Nick Faldo was in contention in the field behind me, and I went on to place one of my best drives straight down the middle of the fairway, hit my second shot to within 40 yards of the green, and made birdie to increase my lead by one stroke over Faldo, while Langer made double-bogey.

Now compare my performance then with the memorable duel between Ernie Els and Colin Montgomerie during the 1994 World Matchplay Championship at Wentworth. As you will remember, the leading Els placed his ball in the bunker of the 15th hole. To the utter amazement of the gallery, Montgomerie who was one stroke behind, then proceeded to follow Els into the sand trap. At that stage, the game was over for Montgomerie. What drove Montgomerie into the bunker, was, of course, not so much his driver as his state of mind. Confidence has incredible impact on anyone's game whether amateur or professional, but more so on the drive than on other shots.

The drama of the tee shot greatly outweighs any other aspect of the game. A new hole is before you like a new chance. Past mishits are forgotten and forgiven. Your drive now can set you up for a brilliant score or a disaster. More often than not you also find the next group behind you adding to the tension. Only you know if you can hit the driver with confidence under these circumstances.

The driver is both the most difficult club to hit and the club you hit most - with the exception of the putter. The low degree of loft makes it difficult for some amateurs to impart the right amount of backspin to get the ball up in the air, while at the same time the lack of loft makes it easy to impart an extra amount of unwanted sidespin, resulting in a deviation from the intended line of flight. The long shaft, usually some 43 inches, causes the club to travel on a wider arc. Overcoming these difficulties and generating power and precision off the tee requires perfect timing.

The Maximum Distance

The photographs on the following pages were taken with a special swing sequence camera that shoots 75 frames in one second. In other words, it takes a picture every 0.0133 second. From the beginning to the end of any of my swings, Leonard Kamsler recorded 135 photographs, which translates into a swing speed of 1.7955 seconds. It takes me 0.3724 seconds to carry the club from the address position to waist height; this is obviously the slowest part, since it accounts for about one-fifth of the total swing time, while the clubhead travels less than one-sixth of the way.

Almost half the time I spend on my entire swing is taken up by my backswing. I need a total of 0.6916 seconds to reach the top, where I pause with the club perfectly in position for about 0.0533 seconds. From there it only takes me 0.2793 seconds, or one-sixth of the total, to reach impact. I slow down again tremendously during the top part of the follow through.

The timing was the same during each of the twelve swing sequences Leonard photographed for us, regardless of the clubs I used, which ran from a driver to a sand wedge. I must admit that I was rather relaxed when we took those photographs. I enjoyed hitting balls on the delightful Medalist course under the

chest about 15 degrees to clear the way for a strong impact. The back of my left hand and the club face are squared to the target. Notice the relaxed position of the left foot. The right heel is down and ahead of the toes. I extend my arms fully to the left side and my right arm crosses over the left through impact. As the right shoulder comes under the chin, the hands release and follow the ball. PAGES 48 AND 49: The body has now released. My belt buckle points at the target and my shoulders have reached a position well past perpendicular to the pin. Notice how little of my weight is left on my right foot as I have released all my power to my left side in a classic finish.

October sun. There was no pressure on me then, and it is likely that the speed with which I swing increases slightly in major tournaments. However, my rhythm - the time ratio between the individual parts and the whole swing always remains the same.

It so happens that the swing I am most comfortable with is a matter of barely two seconds, but there is nothing hasty in it since I don't use my power potential to the limit. Rhythm and balance account for most of the precision and consistency of my drives - and some of their length - because it allows me to accelerate through impact.

Even if your swing rhythm is not as fast-paced as mine, the proportionate time I spend on takeaway, backswing, pause, impact, and follow through gives you a good guideline to follow to create a well-balanced timing for your swing. It usually helps your rhythm if you start slowing down.

Don't hurry your swing by hitting at 100 percent of your capacity. I don't do it, because I would lose control over my swing. I hit probably at 80 percent of my strength - no more. This allows me to release my hands naturally and easily at impact, and to deliver the sweet spot of the clubhead to the ball. If you generate tremendous clubhead speed at impact and mishit the shot because you can't control it properly, your entire effort is wasted.

By all means, go ahead and try it. Hit a couple of balls on the driving range at your full capacity. Most likely, the results will stun you - though not by the distance you generate but rather by the sizable area your balls cover. Even if - by some miraculous intervention from above - you should be pleased with the results, you cannot generate these consistently. So, slow down.

I know it is difficult to believe that slowing down will increase your clubhead speed or the length of your drives. But I don't stand alone with this advice. One of the longest hitters on the Tour, Jack Nicklaus, is renowned for his slow takeaway. Whenever he wants to hit an extra long shot, he makes an extra slow takeaway. I do the same. It works.

As a drill, try to take the club away very slowly. At the waist-high position, the club shaft is in line with the feet to set up for a perfect extension on the backswing. The weight has shifted more to the right leg, and the wrists have not yet cocked. Take a conscious break on top of the backswing, and let the dynamics of your swing carry the clubhead through impact when you next hit balls on the range. You will rediscover the rhythm that works best for you, and the immediate results will be an easy swing and long, straight shots. You should then work through your bag to adapt your rhythm to all the clubs and shots you hit.

50

Rhythm determines how effectively your clubhead will be delivered to the ball. Timing allows you to release your hands and wrists consciously at impact. To accelerate through impact, move your hips by 30 degrees and your shoulders by 15 degrees to the left before impact to make way for your arms, and keep your head behind the ball through impact. The head position is important because it balances you through impact and ensures that your hands release a little before the clubhead actually hits the ball, sending it on a higher trajectory.

A wide swing arc is essential to generate enough clubhead speed to hit a powerful drive. There is no denying it - you need to be fit and flexible to make a long shoulder turn, with a minimal hip turn and a firmly grounded left heel against the anchor of your right leg. Trained muscles and flexible joints allow you to rotate your upper body until your back is at least squared to the target. Your left arm must remain almost straight at the top of the swing to add tension to your body coil and retain the widest possible swing arc. Throughout your entire swing, one arm stays always stretched.

The unwinding of, first, the lower and, second, the upper body from such a position produces such enormous clubhead speed at impact that its momentum carries you through to a finish facing the target. Stretches in the gym or during your favorite sports activity will help you to rotate further and gain yardage on your drives.

Concentrate on consistency and precision - not length - by working on your weight transfer, the balance, and the timing. After all, my esteemed fellow-countryman Peter Thomson managed to win five British Open titles and many others despite his relatively short drives. This talented golfer catches up with the long hitters just by driving straight down the middle of the fairway, on hole after hole after hole.

Mind you, there is no honor in driving off a tee if your three-wood does the job more accurately and consistently. To know what you can do and to know what you cannot is a great gift in golf. I advise you to fine-tune your shotmaking skills with the clubs you can handle comfortably. Remember, even I use my three-wood (or my two-iron, for that matter) off the tee whenever it appears wise to lay off.

The High Drive

The key to all shotmaking is subtlety. When working the ball, very little change is needed to the basic swing. These nuances are not difficult to execute, but to know with certainty just how much difference results in exactly the trajectory you want to achieve requires years of practice.

RIGHT: *You can see clearly that my weight is concentrated on my left side through impact, with the left knee less flexed than the right. This imbalance is one of the keys to a powerful drive as a lot of weight can then be transferred through impact.* OPPOSITE, RIGHT: *My weight has shifted to the outside of my left foot as the clubhead reaches its highest point, but my head has remained behind the movement for a better balance.* FAR RIGHT: *The weight has now completely shifted to my left foot. The knees have rotated to face the target squarely and the right shoulder points to the target. A follow through cannot be faked as the clubhead speed carries your hands and arms through it. Your finish is a telltale sign for the balance of your swing. A less than perfect follow through will cost you shot distance and height.*

RIGHT: *My knees are well flexed at address. My arms hang down comfortably without being stretched forward to the ball. The angle of the club shaft indicates the correct distance to the ball. At the waist-high position, the club shaft is in line with the feet. This allows for a perfect extension on the backswing.*

OPPOSITE, RIGHT: *The right knee has rotated to the right and the weight has shifted more to my right leg on the takeaway. The arms are still stretched, and the wrists have not yet cocked.*

BELOW RIGHT: *You can clearly see that the left knee is much more flexed than the right, indicating the weight transfer.* FAR RIGHT: *At the top of the swing, I have produced a full shoulder turn, with minimal hip turn to increase the tension in the body coil for a powerful release. The right leg has retained its posture to anchor the swing. My left arm has remained almost straight. Notice, how little the wrists are bent in this position.* BELOW FAR RIGHT: *The weight shift is more pronounced, the left knee has flexed further, and my belt buckle has turned 45 degrees away from the address position.*

When you need a higher than normal drive - to clear a group of trees on a dog-leg corner off the tee, for instance - move the ball up in your stance just a little so that it lies opposite the ball of your left foot rather than its heel. Doing so has, in effect, moved your head behind the ball, allowing your head to stay back as you swing through long enough to square the club face at impact and through it. This is of vital importance since the ball leaves at right angles to loft and the alignment of the club face through impact. This head position also causes you to release your hands a little earlier than during your normal swing which allows you to throw the ball up in the air better. The swing itself remains unchanged.

As the impact zone - due to the changed ball position - has now moved forward from the bottom of the swing arc, you also need to tee the ball up higher so that the sweet spot on the club face is delivered right through the ball. The adjustment, again, is minute. I usually tee up a ball at roughly one and a half inches from the turf for the driver. For a high ball, I add half an inch at the most.

The Low Drive

For a drive with a low trajectory, move the ball a fraction back in the stance from its usual position opposite your left heel so that the clubhead catches the ball before it reaches the lowest point of the swing arc. The altered ball position allows you to impart a shallow blow at the ball to trim the backspin; and less backspin results in a flatter trajectory. The ball leaves the club face at a right angle after impact, straight and low, if you push the tee down by about half an inch or a quarter inch. Retain more of your weight on your left side during the backswing to avoid hitting a high trajectory.

As you can see in the photographs on page 59, the swing for the low-flying shot is drastically different from my normal swing pattern. My stance is wider than normal for a slightly flatter and wider swing both on the backswing and follow through. The wide waist-high position during the takeaway is mirrored exactly in the follow through. The shallow downswing into the ball imparts power and speed to the ball without making it soar. The result is a nice low trajectory.

The Fade

To fade a ball, align your body about 20 degrees to the left of the target, with the club face facing the target. The more you open your club face and stance, the more the ball will curve and the shorter the ball will fly. As you can see in the photograph on page 60 in the waist-high position, the club moves back parallel to the feet. When I now swing, the club hits through the ball with an open face and thus creates the left to right line of flight. The ball starts out parallel to my foot alignment and finishes where I have aimed the club face. You must fade the ball with your body, not your hands.

The Draw

To hit a draw, align your feet about 20 degrees right of the target, drawing the right foot back behind the left by approximately two inches. The club face is squared to the target but closed in relation to the alignment of your feet. Take the club back parallel to your stance – in other words, outside the target line – and swing along the line of your feet. This action results in a closed club face at impact, allowing the club to turn over just a little to the left. The ball will gently curve from right to left. As with the fade, you use your body, not your hands to draw the ball.

The Driving Mistakes

As I explained earlier, shotmaking skill requires very fine adjustments. Finding the exact ball position is one of those. A poor ball position creates a bad backswing and ruins your shot.

A ball that is placed too far forward in your stance affects your swing. The club will no longer point to your left armpit. You will also notice that your hands fall behind the ball position. If you ever saw a side view of the same set-up you would realize that your chest and shoulder are aligned as if you had an open stance, with your shoulders turned around to the left to reach the ball. However, since your feet are aligned to the target, the body is already twisted at address. The result is predictable. You now have no choice but to initiate a takeaway to the outside.

On the other hand, a swing attempt with a ball position that has been moved too far behind will move your hands slightly in front of the ball, while your head stays behind. The closed stance that this ball position forces on the player forces a takeaway from inside-out.

The ball position will also result in a downward blow on the ball, creating a shallow departure of the ball from the club face since it has in effect been delofted at impact.

THE HIGH DRIVE

ABOVE AND RIGHT: *The ball position has moved up in the stance by an inch and the ball is teed up half an inch higher.* **ABOVE RIGHT:** *A full turn behind the ball creates a larger weight transfer to the right leg and increases the power on the downswing. You should rotate your shoulders until they are at least perpendicular to the target.* **ABOVE FAR RIGHT:** *On the downswing, try to release the club earlier than normal. The head position behind the ball has effectively moved the center of gravity back in the stance. You will naturally release when the clubhead swings through the bottom of your swing arc which is in line with your head. The clubhead will be released before it reaches the ball.*

58

FAR LEFT AND BELOW LEFT: *For the low drive, you need to push the ball back in the stance by an inch and the tee down.* **LEFT:** *A little more weight remains on the left side during the backswing than on a normal shot. This more balanced weight position ensures that less power and backspin is imparted on the ball through impact, preventing a high trajectory. The swing is shorter and flatter, both on the backswing and the follow through.*

DRIVING A FADE

RIGHT: *My stance is open, with my shoulders aiming to the left of the target. The club face is aimed at the target.* BELOW RIGHT: *Take the club back in line with the feet. This set up creates a left-to-right shot with a normal swing.*

LEFT: *For a draw, align
your feet about 20 degrees to
right of the target, drawing
the right foot behind the left.
The club face is squared to
the target.* BELOW LEFT:
*Take the club back in line
with the feet and swing as
you normally would.*

THE FAIRWAY WOODS

Once you have stepped down from the tee box, your swing arc becomes steeper by a few degrees because the ball is lying lower. The shafts of your clubs become shorter and you move closer to the ball. In other words, most of the difficulties golfers experience with drivers have suddenly disappeared. A shorter swing is more easily balanced than a longer one, and the shorter shaft lets you work the ball more subtly.

Whenever the distance of your drives may land you in trouble - at a river running through the fairway, a dog-leg corner blocking your way, or a large-looming sand trap within range - lay up with your woods. On the tee box, their big sole is no liability, and all their advantages over the driver are in play.

You can't birdie par five's and long par four's without mastering your fairway woods. As a matter of fact, one of my favorite memories in golf is the three-wood I fired 243 yards across the water to an island green on the 18th hole during the final round of the1992 Canadian Open.

However, fairway woods require a lot of control. You can never pick up a ball from the fairway with a wood quite as cleanly as you can with an iron. The big sole of the fairway wood - an advantage in the rough - tends to create too much friction with grass and soil to allow for finesse, and the comparatively longer shaft moves you literally one step further from tight control. It is furthermore difficult to impart just the right amount of backspin on the ball with a wood.

Because of the thickness of their sole, the better manicured the fairway, the more accurate the wood shot. Therefore, let me caution you not to attempt too many changes to the line of flight at the same time. Unless you have practiced those shots intensively, it can be very testing to produce a low fade or a high draw with a wood, for instance.

As a seasoned golfer, you should cram a four- or a five-wood together with your three-wood into your bag.

Personally, I much prefer to hit a long iron down the fairway than any of these because I can pick the ball crisply off the fairway and control its flight better. But the woods have an advantage over the irons in medium-high rough, where the sole of the woods helps to press the weeds and grass down instead of getting entangled as an iron might.

The Three-Wood

The three-wood is probably the one club golfers enjoy hitting most. Since the shaft of the fairway wood is on average two inches shorter than that of the driver, the club is more manageable. The slightly reduced swing arc produced by the three-wood restricts the amount of clubhead speed you can generate with it. But this disadvantage should be offset by the lighter clubhead, with a sole that allows you to hit the club out of the rough as well.

When setting up for a three-wood shot, stand with the inside of your feet roughly shoulder-width apart, an inch less so than for the driver. Keep your knees well flexed to allow you to turn in spite of the width of your stance which restricts your hip turn. The tension between a restricted hip turn and a wide shoulder rotation results in a powerful release.

Position the ball opposite your left armpit, in line with your left heel. Again, your left foot should point about 20 degrees to the left so that you can move the left side of your body out of the way quickly for a speedy acceleration of the club through the impact zone.

Don't tee up higher than about an inch from the ground for your three-wood, and a quarter inch less for the shorter woods. The height of the tee will have flattened your swing arc again, so that it even more closely resembles your drive. On the fairway, your swing arc is steeper and you can impart more backspin on the ball than you did off the tee. As a consequence, the ball will fly higher and roll less. The friction of the thick sole of the wood will slow your clubhead speed through impact, and you will lose additional length on the shot.

The fairway shot is slightly more difficult than the tee shot with the same club as the tee allows you to catch the ball well on the upswing. The clubhead actually brushes the turf at the bottom of the swing arc, which is closer to the center of your stance, before it hits the ball on the tee. When you hit off the fairway, you don't have this advantage, and the club face will hit the ball slightly closer to its equator than near its bottom. If the greenkeeper has not mowed too closely, the grass will help you to cushion the ball, and you stand to hit a better fairway shot. On a very low-cut turf, you are better off hitting an iron.

Your arms and hands should hang down straight from your shoulders at address. This means that, because of the shorter shaft, you should also stand probably an inch closer to the ball than you did teeing off with the driver. The clubhead should hover behind the ball when you hit your three-wood off the tee or off the fairway to avoid building up any tension in your arms and wrists.

THE FAIRWAY WOODS

RIGHT: *The set up for the three-wood is slightly narrower than for the driver.* FAR RIGHT: *The clubhead brushes the turf during the takeaway along the target line.* OPPOSITE, RIGHT: *The weight has shifted to the inside of the right leg and the foot and the club face has left the alignment to the target to be rotated to the right.* FAR RIGHT: *The clubhead has been lifted off the ground, but the arms are still extended straight, the wrists have not cocked and the triangle between arms and shoulders is intact.* THIS PAGE, BELOW RIGHT: *Prior to impact, the wrists are uncocking. Both heels are firmly on the ground, while the weight is still concentrated on the right foot for a powerful stroke. Note that the head is positioned behind the ball.* OPPOSITE, BELOW RIGHT AND BELOW FAR RIGHT: *Because of the length of the three-wood shaft, I use a more sweeping motion with my swing. There is no need to help the ball into the air; the loft will do that automatically. A smooth rhythmic swing is all that it takes.*

Take the club away low and slow for a powerful hit with the wood. Let the clubhead of the wood travel along the target line initially, until your arms have reached their furthest extension to the right. The weight then starts to shift to the right as you begin the takeaway.

Maintain the triangle formed by your arms and chest as long as you can to set up for a wide shoulder turn and safeguard against an early cocking (vertically) and hinging (horizontally) of your wrists. If you start bending your wrists before the club reaches the waist-high position - where the club should be in line with your feet to allow for a good extension on the backswing - you will set up for a steep swing plane, which will prevent the sweeping blow you need to impart on the ball with the woods.

At the top of the swing, your left knee will have turned to the right, while most of your weight is concentrated on the less flexed right leg. This serves as an anchor to your swing. Your hips should rotate about 35 degrees and your left shoulder about 100 degrees until it points to the right of the ball, or as far as you can reach. Stretch your arms out behind your head, rather than above it, to maintain the flat swing plane necessary for the sweeping blow of the woods. Keep your left arm, as well as your wrists, almost straight. Stop the club before it reaches parallel to the ground, and make sure that your weight does not shift past the center of the right foot. You will then be able to hit a long and straight fairway wood.

To start the downswing, transfer the weight back to the left foot. The previous weight imbalance is one of the keys to a powerful drive, allowing a lot of weight to be transferred before and during impact. Retain your head behind the movement for balance and to make it easy for you to release early while keeping the clubhead squared through impact.

Rotate your hips to the left until they point 35 degrees to the left of the target. Your chest should be turned 15 degrees to the left as well to allow you to drop your arms and hands naturally and accelerate through impact as your right shoulder comes under your chin. The back of your left hand and the club face should be squared not only at impact but also through it to sweep the ball off the fairway with an upward movement of the clubhead.

Extend your arms fully and let your right arm cross over the left on the follow through. Your ball will fly off on a low trajectory at first, due to the low loft of the three-wood, but will gain height subsequently. There is not much backspin on the ball because of the wide and shallow swing arc, and it will roll long.

On the follow through, your hips and shoulders should turn as far as they did on the backswing. The weight transfer to the left side continues, and the centrifugal force of your swing should carry you to a powerful finish.

The Tee Shot

Before you start hitting your tee shot down the middle with your wood or working your club to shape a sideways spin into your trajectory, you should have gathered information about the course, the designer, the grass and weather conditions you are playing on, and the particular hole you are at.

The scorecard gives you some indication on the layout and yardage, but it rarely tells you about the undulations, slopes and ridges on and about the fairway, or the rugged wasteland stretches you may find bisecting the holes (frequently seen on courses in Scotland and in my home country, Australia). A low index of the hole is usually a warning of trouble lurking ahead. Designers often have their own particular trademarks which they leave on a course. Knowing their idiosyncrasies helps decide on your play. Tap local knowledge wherever you can, from your playing partner, caddie or the greenkeeper.

Once on the tee box, take the bearings around you. Where are the boundaries of the fairway? What is the general line of the hole? What does the tree line tell you about the slopes ahead? Are there any ponds or rivulets to avoid? Where is out-of-bounds? And where are the bunkers? Pick your target on the fairway, imagine the highest point in your planned trajectory and aim your shot there.

The length and width of the fairway below is difficult to gauge on an elevated tee box. The height will let your ball fly further, meaning that it will go further into trouble if you mishit your shot, so select a club off the tee that ensures you hit straight. The elevation will take care of the distance.

If the fairway is towering above you, a driver may also not be your preferred choice. The uphill slope will stop a stray shot most of the time before it veers off into the out-of-bounds or falls into a ravine. On the other hand, a fairway wood with its greater loft – or even a long iron – will get your ball into the air before it bounces into the incline.

Lastly, check the tee box before you tee up. Is it aligned to the hole? Does it slant? Are the tee markers in line with the direction of your shot? Does any corner of the tee reveal a different angle of the hole and offer you an alternative avenue for attack? Pick the side where trouble looms and hit away from it. By now, you should have a very good idea of your preferred landing area off the tee, and be able to choose the club that will see you there safely.

OVERLEAF: *The swing arc for the three-wood is almost as long as for the driver. The shoulders turn right back until they are well past perpendicular to the target, and the leg drive is mighty. The knee rotation describes almost a quarter-circle throughout the swing. The right elbow starts to straighten as the club comes down. Through impact, the clubhead, straightened arms and the head all form one line. The head is still focused on the impact zone. The right foot, knee, and hip are still rotating until the follow through is completed.*

THE LONG IRONS

Getting a better grip on long iron performance is probably the biggest challenge for seasoned golfers, since they are the basic shotmaking tools on the fairway. You will not be able to finesse approach shots on long par four's or short par five's without hitting your basic long iron shots well.

Start with the longest iron you are comfortable with, such as a three- or four-iron, and practice your way up from there. Begin by choking down on the shaft to get a better grip on the club and by hitting nothing more than half-swings. This is a great exercise to get a good feel for the clubs.

Once your long irons appear less forbidding, progress to a three-quarter swing and eventually a full swing. Do not introduce any more changes to your usual swing than required by the different shaft length. Most of all - maintain your rhythm.

You will find, indeed, that the difficulty with long irons lies predominantly in the head. Mistakes, of course, are aggravated by the very little underspin and the amount of undesirable sidespin imparted by the low-lofted long irons. The low loft of the long irons also makes it difficult to get the ball up into the air.

Since the golf ball always departs at right angles to the loft of the club face through impact, the initial trajectory of the long irons is shallow. But long irons are not the only clubs with low lofts. You should always bear in mind that the driver has a lower loft than even the one-iron. So, if you can hit your driver, you can hit long irons, too.

With a driver, your main concern is distance. To generate more distance for your shots, all woods require a sweeping blow when you hit them off the tee or off the fairway. This in turn affects their bite. The more sweeping your blow, the less backspin you will impart on a ball, resulting in a lower trajectory of the ball and a longer roll.

By contrast, a long iron shot is an approach shot, requiring both length and precision. You probably need your long iron shot to stop on a slippery green and not shoot right across it. In other words, you are looking for some backspin on your ball.

I am not saying that a long iron shot can stop dead on its track on the putting surface or spin back towards the pin, but it should have enough backspin on it to allow better placement than a wood shot. Why? The reason is that you are standing closer to the ball, in a more upright position which allows you to create a steeper swing plane. A steep swing arc results in more backspin on the ball and a higher trajectory.

However, in spite of the steeper and slightly curtailed swing arc, you are still dealing the ball a sweeping blow at impact. The adjustments made in your stance are small in relation to the length of the club. It is a steeper sweeping blow, admittedly, than the one you hit with the woods, but it is by no means a descending blow. Only the sweeping blow ensures that you generate the distance you need from a long iron shot.

A descending blow imparts too much backspin on the ball to reach the green, as it were. If you have a close look at the pictures on page 74, you will notice that I sweep the long iron shots clean off the fairway. You won't find the merest trace of a divot.

The turning point between the sweeping and the descending blow comes with the mid irons which require a swing somewhere between these two options. I like to pick the mid iron ball off the fairway. The short irons are really the ones requiring the descending blow, with a divot, most of the time.

Before you dart off to the nearest pro shop to purchase your new two-iron, check your current equipment if you don't know the swing weight of your clubs offhand. Some equipment may be less suited to match the rest of your clubs than others.

Long irons have less weight in the club heads; this can affect their swing weight. The lighter the clubhead in relation to shaft and grip, the lower the swing weight of the club. The swing weight of long irons may be light and, consequently, their shafts may appear stiff. A lighter swing weight also ruins your feel for the club. Make sure that you purchase clubs with a swing weight matching the clubs in your bag.

Another problem area is frequency-matching. The vibration of the individual clubs should be matched to each other so that the clubs react to the swing in more or less the same way. It is worth checking swing weight and frequency throughout your set if you have problems with individual clubs. Faults in the equipment are magnified in long iron play as these clubs are the least forgiving of any set.

The Two-Iron

A long iron provides an excellent alternative to a three-wood off the tee and on the fairway. It does not have to be a one-iron, though. Very few players I know are 100 percent comfortable hitting a one-iron. Even I don't carry one any more.

I use the two-iron most, both on and off the tee-boxes. Its shaft is shorter by about half an inch than that of a one-iron and its loft a little more, so I have better control over the club. With a respectable 250 yards, it also gives me more distance than most people get from their drives.

The key to hitting the long irons lies in not trying to hit them hard. A big shoulder turn and a restricted hip rotation will do the trick. For more distance, set up with a faintly wider stance, so that your hip turn is limited further. This will increase the tension between your upper and lower body, when you complete your shoulder turn.

Because of the shorter shaft of the two-iron, stand two or three inches closer to the ball at address and narrow your stance by as much compared to the three-wood address. You now stand more upright and produce a steeper swing arc.

The obvious alternative is to tilt the waist more to reach the ball with the clubhead, but such a posture only leads to a flatter swing arc and a shallow trajectory for the ball. This posture will also cause problems placing your shots.

Set up for the long irons just as you do for the woods, with your left foot still pointing 20 degrees to the left. It is paramount for hitting the long irons to accelerate through impact to get a reasonable result out of your shot. Get ready to move the left side of your body clear of the impact zone in time.

Your ball position should still be in line with your left heel and your left armpit so that it is inevitably hit on the upswing. Let the clubhead hover behind the ball at address for a long and slow takeaway. Slowing down helps you accelerate, remember?

Due to the shorter shaft of the iron, your swing arc is not only steeper but also slightly shorter, resulting in more control over the shot. The shorter swing arc marginally reduces the knee rotation and weight transfer, compared to the woods. However, try to turn your shoulder generously until it reaches at least perpendicular to the target line. Clamp down on your hip turn, which should not surpass 30 degrees on the backswing.

OPPOSITE: *The secret to hitting good solid long irons is in not trying to hit them too hard. A big shoulder and hip turn is almost all it takes. Stop the club before it reaches parallel to the ground without allowing your wrists to collapse at the top of the backswing. Let the centrifugal force of your swing carry your arms through impact to a long follow through. If you make solid contact, the ball will jump off the club face because of the lack of loft on the long irons.*

THE LONG IRONS

RIGHT: *The takeaway is similar to that for the driver. You have to set up for a long, sweeping hit into the ball, with your legs fairly wide apart, though not quite as much as for the driver. Your knees are well-flexed and the waist tilted.* CENTER RIGHT: *A low wide takeaway starts the swing.* FAR RIGHT: *The ball position is the same as for the driver - opposite the left armpit.* OVERLEAF: *The arc is wide, with a full shoulder turn. The weight shifts to the right leg, as the left shoulder turns behind the ball. The left arm is stretched to the utmost, and the left elbow points down and behind at the top of the backswing because of the powerful shoulder rotation.*

74

So, make sure that your knees are well flexed at address; otherwise your upper body cannot turn freely. The more pliable your knees, the easier it will be for you to keep your left heel on the ground.

At the top of your swing, about 60 percent of your weight should be on your right foot.

Don't let your wrists collapse at the top of your swing and stop the club just a hint before it reaches the top position of the driver and the three-wood. Try to consciously feel the club reach this position. If you keep your mind focused on it, you will have no problems controlling your club face on the downswing and through impact, even though you have only a small club face to deal with moving at about 120 miles per hour.

You can practice this by making your backswing with your eyes closed; you can then concentrate on feeling it better. Once you think the club is in position, ask your playing partner to check, if you can't practice in front of a mirror. Your elbow should still be pointing down and back at the top to show you that the shoulder turn was wide and complete.

On the downswing, which starts with a slight lateral leg drive to the left to initiate the weight transfer, move your hips by about 30 degrees and your shoulders by about 15 degrees out of the way of your arms, prior to impact, to be able to accelerate properly through impact. Pin your right elbow close to your body and uncock (horizontally) and unhinge (vertically) your wrists gradually as your body rotates from right to left. This way, you will be able to hit your long irons with precision.

The centrifugal force of your swing will carry you through impact. You need to keep your right leg almost passive and your head behind the ball at impact to facilitate an early release of your hands, generating more distance for your shot. The wide swing arc must be completed by a long follow through.

The High, Soft Shot

High, soft long iron shots require expertise and practice to be executed properly. Move the ball up in your stance by an inch, so that it lies opposite the ball of your left foot, just as you do for a high drive. This ball position pushes your head and the vertical axis of your swing arc behind the ball. Your head stays back through impact and your hands release at the bottom of your swing arc, which is in line with your head. By the time the clubhead meets the ball, you are on the upswing, throwing the ball up in the air.

LEFT AND FAR LEFT: *The downswing starts from the ground up. You can see here how the weight is transferred back to the left side as my left shoulder rotates to the left. The left leg stretches into a straighter position while turning left, whereas the right knee begins to flex more the further it rotates to the left.* **BELOW LEFT AND BELOW FAR LEFT:** *Notice the position of my right elbow close to my body and the gradual uncocking of the wrists in the photographic sequence on this page . There is a little lateral leg drive to start the downswing.* **OVERLEAF:** *As with the driver, notice how passive my right foot is. Both heels are firmly planted on the ground. The only action as the body rotates from right to left stems from the wrists which are uncocking (vertically), and unhinging (horizontally) to square the club face at impact.* **FOLLOWING PAGES:** *Notice my head position well behind the ball through impact - not only at impact. The sweeping blow at the ball took the merest divot.*

For a high drive, I tee up to make allowance for the relocated impact zone which no longer is at the lowest point of the swing arc. For the high, soft long iron off the turf, the ball position causes a problem. The ball is hit slightly closer to the leading edge of the club face rather than with the center of the club. In other words, the sweet spot for the high shot off the fairway is marginally reduced. This adds much to the difficulty of executing this shot, especially with the problematic long irons.

The Low, Running Shot

A flat, long, running ball is a shot I thoroughly enjoy hitting, particularly into the wind on those magnificent rough and rugged old Scottish golf courses. This shot has often saved me strokes on the wind-swept European Tour, and its execution has become second nature to me.

Similar to hitting a low drive, move the ball a fraction back in the stance so that it lies right inside your left heel. Again, shorten your swing for the low-flying shot to almost three-quarters and flatten the angle so that the swing arc remains wide - for distance - and becomes shallow - for the intended trajectory.

Remember that the ball always departs at a right angle from the loft of the club face when the ball leaves the club head through impact. In other words, the steeper your swing through impact, the more backspin you impart on the ball and the higher it soars, and the flatter you sweep it away, the less backspin it receives and the lower it flies. You have to stay down and keep your head behind the ball through impact.

In the gales of British links courses, I even grip down on the shaft by one or one-and-a-half inches to let the ball bore better through the wind and hold its line. Another option is to draw a shot with a flatter swing arc, if the terrain allows it, because a left-to-right spin will usually cause the ball to fly low and roll a lot after landing.

The Long-Iron Mistakes

The problems inherent with using long irons lead to a series of blatant mistakes which afflict beginners and advanced players alike. Ask your club professional or playing partner to analyze your swing pattern if your long irons are causing trouble. You, too, may be guilty of posture offenses, to some degree.

The margin for error with the long irons is extremely small because of the lack of loft and the thin club face. Therefore it is crucial to make solid contact with the ball at impact. Whenever golfers doubt their ability to get the ball up in the air with these clubs, they attempt to steer the ball upwards.

This usually results in standing up on the shot on the downswing and at impact, resulting in a strike at the ball low on the club face; in other words, a top. Golfers with this posture also don't swing through the shot but finish high. If you tend to top your ball with long irons, this may be your fault.

Other frequent mistakes include forcing the club and over-swinging, again in an attempt to gain distance and uplift. A close look at the place and the depth of your divots will tell you if you have been trying to blast the ball away by hitting from the top with your hands, or if your clubhead has left your swing path. There will also be a lot of soil sticking to your club face that shouldn't be there.

The long iron shots require no divot at all as you are sweeping the ball off the fairway just as you do a wood. A smooth, easy swing is really all that is needed; the loft of long irons hit well will get the ball airborne.

THE MID IRONS

As you move through your set from the driver to the wedges, clubs become more easily manageable. This is because the greater loft of the club face imparts greater backspin on the ball, reducing the effect of sidespin on it. The middle irons offer versatile shotmaking for approaches on par fours which require shaping shots into the greens, around dog-legs, through the wind, out of the rough and across the slopes on the green.

If you can shape the trajectory of your approach shot both vertically and horizontally, you will gain control of the angle with which your ball lands on the green and, as a result, its bounce and roll on the ground.

The Approach Shots

When planning an approach strategy, always start your ball wide of the target, curving its trajectory towards it. It is usually not a good idea to strike a mid iron right at the pin. A straight shot may bounce off a hard surface and roll through the green or it may stop dead in wet soil short of it. The terrain may be sloping and deviate your straight ball away from the pin.

You may also have a natural tendency to fade or draw which could land your ball pin-high if you aim straight at the flag, only to have it spin away from the target.

Working your approach shot as close to the hole as possible requires the consideration of all factors affecting the target area. These include the weather, the terrain, the hazards, the shape of the green, the undulations on the green, the quality and cut of the grass, and the pin position.

As a rule of thumb, whenever the pin is in the left hand side of the green, I draw the ball to the pin. The ball hits the green near the middle and the ball's right-to-left spin will take it to the hole. It is obviously important to know the exact amount of roll a draw will generate. The distance is longer than that of a fade since the trajectory of a draw is lower. By letting the ball land right in the center of the green, normally the biggest landing area, I allow myself a wide safety margin for the roll.

If the pin is on the right side of the green, I normally hit a fade. The trajectory of the ball will be higher, and the roll less. Hazards or the shape of the green may, of course, force a change in plan, but the principle is always to pick the safest, widest landing area away from trouble spots and to let the spin propel the ball towards the pin. Your mastering of high and low draws and fades with your mid irons sets up many birdie opportunities.

The Regular Mid Iron Shot

The shorter shafts of the mid irons require slight adjustments in your stance. You need to stand closer to the ball at address and to tilt your waist more. In this way, the plane of your swing arc will not change from the long iron shots. If you have kept the correct swing arc angle, your divots should be as small as those of your long irons.

Leave the ball in the usual position, so that you can hit the mid irons on the upswing as you hit the longer clubs. The mid irons do not ask for a descending blow on the ball but because of the shorter length of their shafts, you will pick the ball off the fairway rather than sweep it away.

It is essential to place your approach shots accurately near the pin with your mid irons, meaning you require a lot of control over your shots. For the optimal placement in your shots, narrow your stance by approximately two inches or more until you feel very comfortable in your address position. Your knees need to be flexed to allow for a slightly shortened shoulder turn, and your weight distributed evenly between your feet.

I have heard of coaches and professional golfers who start their mid iron swing by putting 60 percent of their weight on their left foot and 40 percent on their right foot. For their short iron address, those players even put 70 percent of their weight on their left foot and 30 percent on their right foot. I don't believe that this position can be the basis for a solid, consistent swing. Furthermore, this weight distribution must lead to a more downward blow on the ball, delofting your club and imparting more backspin on your mid iron shot than you need.

For the mid iron shot, your takeaway engages the arms initially more than the shoulders because of the shorter shaft. At the waist-high position, however, the hips have turned by about 15 degrees to the right from the address position, while the shoulders have rotated by 35 degrees. The weight has shifted to the inside of the right leg and foot, and the wrists just start to cock. Extend your arms well and make an almost full shoulder turn. At the top of the swing, your shoulders should have turned 90 degrees to the right, and your left leg should hold less than 25 percent of your weight. However, stop your club well before it reaches parallel to the ground to stay in control of the clubhead.

The lateral leg drive to start the downswing is limited, but the hips begin their rotation to the left until they have turned 35 degrees and the chest 15 degrees to

THE MID IRONS

RIGHT: *The stance is not quite as wide as the one for the long irons but the ball position is the same.* BELOW RIGHT: *My waist tilts a little more to allow for the shorter shaft. The swing arc stays on the same plane.* FAR RIGHT AND BELOW FAR RIGHT: *Notice the low, wide takeaway and the full shoulder turn.*

the left of the address position to clear the impact zone. The club shaft and right arm come down parallel to the feet. As your right arm straightens, your left arm begins to bend for a full release at impact.

On the follow through, my belt buckle is squared to the target and my shoulders have turned well past it.

The Punch Shot

The punch is an effective shot into a headwind or crosswind, or out of the rough from beneath low branches, for instance. The line of flight of a punch is low, penetrating and shorter than a normal shot with the same club.

To set up a punch shot, move the ball back again so that it comes to rest just an inch inside your left heel, as if hitting a low drive. Again, your weight remains more on your left side than it would on a normal swing. This position should let you feel to be slightly ahead of the ball.

The backswing is short in length; no longer than a three-quarter swing. However, it should be steep, with a sharp and accurate downswing. At impact, my wrist is bowed a little and the club face appears less lofted because of the steep backswing. I hold this position through the ball and thus limit my follow through, keeping the ball low but shortening its flight distance at the same time.

When hitting the punch out of the rough, you need to make a steep downswing, so that the clubhead does not get entangled in the grass.

The Low Fade

The low fade is a complicated shot because a fade spin usually propels the ball upward. To set up for it, move the ball an inch back in the stance as you do for your usual low shot so that it lies right inside your left heel. Your stance is slightly wider than my usual mid iron address; you need a lower center of gravity to allow for a shallower swing arc and a lower follow through.

As you see overleaf, my backswing is so short that it can hardly be called three-quarter. This allows better control over the club face through the ball and better feel for the low trajectory. Of course, the weight transfer is much less pronounced than it would be for a normal mid iron swing.

To shape a curvature of a fade into the flat shot, align your body to the left of the target, but the club face remains facing it. The club is taken back in line

OVERLEAF, LEFT: *A very good extension on the through swing is essential for the distance and direction of the shot. The right arm and the club shaft are in line with the feet, and the club face is square at impact. My hips have turned 35 degrees to the left, and my chest 15 degrees. CENTER: As my right arm straightens, the left arm folds, allowing a good full release of body and arms. My belt buckle is facing the target as the clubhead reaches its highest point on the follow through. Chest and shoulders have turned past the target. RIGHT: My hips have rotated about 15 degrees past the target and my right shoulder points at the target, adding power to the shot. Any follow through is as well-balanced as the swing was, and a good check-point for the rest of your performance.*

89

The photographs opposite give you a close glimpse at my weight transfer during the backswing. OPPOSITE, RIGHT: *Early in the takeaway the weight is still evenly distributed between the two legs, and both knees are flexed to the same extent. The shoulders have barely moved.* FAR RIGHT: *More weight is concentrated on the inside of the right leg as the stronger flex of the left knee indicates. The hips have rotated to the right so that the belt buckle has turned about 15 degrees away from the target line at the waist-high position. The shoulders have rotated approximately 35 degrees to the right. The wrists just start to cock.* BELOW RIGHT: *The left leg is bent even more as the hips are rotated about 30 degrees and 45 degrees to the right of the target line.* BELOW FAR RIGHT: *At the top of the backswing, the left knee should hold less than 25 percent of your weight and turn well to the right to allow your shoulders to rotate until they are perpendicular to the target line.*

with the feet. When you now swing, the club face hits through the ball open and thus shapes the line of flight left to right, while the shallow arc and the ball position assure the low trajectory. It is vital to maintain the open position of the club face through impact and through the bottom of the swing arc. The ball starts out low, parallel to your foot alignment and finishes low, where you have aimed the club face.

The High Fade

The high fade is a simpler shot, since fade and backspin work together well. I set up for a high fade as I would for a usual high shot - by moving the ball up in my stance by a fraction so that it lies between the heel and the ball of my left foot. My head is now again effectively behind the ball, allowing it to stay back through impact and causing an earlier release of the hands. Again, the center of gravity has moved back in my stance behind the ball, which is struck with an upward blow at impact.

To fade the shot, aim your body to the left of the target, but make sure the club face remains square to it. The ball position induces an early release of the hands because the weight stays back through impact, causing a high trajectory, and the open club face shapes the left-to-right curvature into the line of flight.

The Low Draw

A flat, long draw is a perfectly easy shot to hit as backspin and sidespin work together. Similar to hitting a low long iron, move the ball back in the stance so that it lies right in the middle between your feet. Place your hands well ahead of the ball so that the club shaft points towards your left thigh. This set-up has moved the vertical swing axis ahead of the ball so that the clubhead reaches the ball before it travels through the bottom of the swing arc. Again, widen the stance to lower the center of gravity as you did for the low fade. The swing arc is short for control, wide for distance, and shallow for the trajectory.

It is easy to draw the ball a little with this flat swing because a right-to-left spin will usually cause the ball to fly low and roll a lot after landing. To make best use of this natural tendency of the spin, align your feet slightly right of the target, drawing the right foot back behind the left. The club face is squared to the target and closed in relation to your feet alignment. The club is taken back parallel to your stance and swung along the line of your feet, resulting in a closed club face at impact.

Once the club face reaches its original address position, it is squared again to the target. The club turns over a little to the left through impact, and the ball will curve from right to left, while the shallow swing and the ball position produce the low trajectory.

The High Draw

The high draw, like the low fade, combines opposing spin directions. To achieve the intended trajectory, I again move the ball up in my stance by a fraction so that it lies just inside the heel of my left foot. This ball position pushes my head behind the ball where it will remain through impact, facilitating an early release of the hands. My weight will be more on my right foot than it would for normal iron shots, resulting in the high trajectory.

The relocation of the impact zone from the bottom of the swing arc to a higher point causes problems. You hit the ball closer to the leading edge of the clubhead, not with the center. In other words, the sweet spot for the high draw is reduced, and you must keep your head very still through impact.

To curve the draw into the line of flight, the feet again are aligned to the right of the target, with the right foot behind the left. At address, I square the club face to the target, which results in a closed club face position in relation to my stance. The takeaway again follows the alignment of the feet. The closed club face through impact curves the ball from right to left, while the swing and the ball position produce the high trajectory.

The Mid Iron Mistakes

Most mid iron mistakes are caused by faulty weight transfers, problems experienced by beginners and advanced players alike. Low handicappers somehow manage to make enough adjustments in their swing to offset a wrong weight transfer, with often astonishing results. However, they would benefit more from correcting the basic fault than from trying to thwart its symptoms.

In a reverse pivot, the weight remains on the left foot, the shoulders tilt instead of turn, and force the head forward. As a result, the ball will fly short and high.

If the shoulder does not turn, the golfer slides sideways in his stance, blocking his right side and preventing it from rotating backwards. A sway often results in a hook, if you stay behind on the downswing. If you sway right on the backswing and left on the downswing, the ball will fly right as the club face is not squared at impact. You will lose direction and distance on your shots.

OPPOSITE, FAR LEFT: *I have started my downswing from the ground up. Coming down, my left knee is still more bent than the right and my left heel is tilted to the right, indicating that most of the weight is concentrated on the right foot. My left arm is stretched, but the right elbow points down and a little back, which is the mark of a powerful and complete backswing. LEFT: The weight is transferred back to the left side, as you can see from the right knee position. The knee has now flexed more, indicating that less weight is concentrated on it, while the less bent left knee is entirely hidden by the right. The belt buckle has all but disappeared from view as my hips rotate to the left to clear the impact zone for hands and arms. Notice the right elbow tucked in closely to the body before the waist-high position of the club for a more controlled shot.*

THE LOW FADE

RIGHT AND BELOW RIGHT: *The ball position is back in the stance and the stance is wider so that you can achieve a lower center of gravity, ensuring a flatter, wider swing arc which is necessary for the low trajectory of the shot. The body is aimed to the left of the target, with the club face pointed at the target to set up for the fade spin.* **ABOVE FAR RIGHT:** *The club is taken back along the line of the feet.* **FAR RIGHT:** *To keep the ball down, the left hand leads the club through impact and the through swing is lower.*

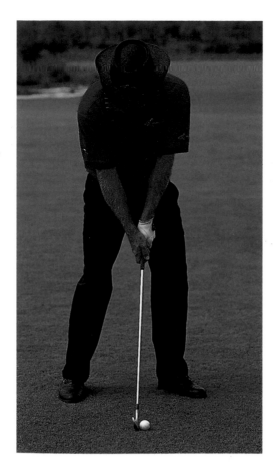

FAR LEFT AND BELOW FAR LEFT: *The body and feet are aimed left of the target, with the ball placed an inch up in the stance. This position allows your hands to release the club a little earlier so that you can contact the ball on the upswing. Your weight should stay back through impact to impart more backspin on the ball for a high trajectory.* **LEFT:** *The follow through is high and complete.*

97

THE LOW DRAW

RIGHT: *The ball is positioned back in the stance and the hands are well ahead of the ball. This set up in effect moves the vertical swing axis ahead of the ball so that the clubhead reaches the ball before it travels through the bottom of the swing arc. The body and feet are closed, aiming to the right of the target. The stance is wider to lower the center of gravity at address and ensure a flatter, wider swing arc.* BELOW: *The club swings back along the line of your feet, but the plane of the arc is flatter both on the backswing and on the follow through. The flat arc will keep the flight of the ball low.*

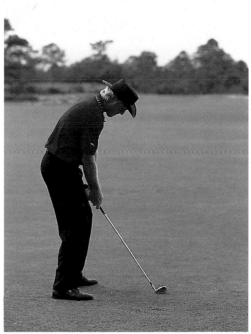

LEFT: *The ball is placed an inch up in the stance. The body and feet are aimed to the right of the target in a closed position at address, with the club face pointing at the target. More weight is concentrated on the right foot than on the left to get the ball up in the air when the weight shifts at impact. The club will release early from this position allowing the ball to be hit higher on the upswing. Your address position creates the draw.*

THE SHORT IRONS

The success of your short iron shots decides the number of putts you have to make throughout a round. On par three's, short par four's and long par five's, a sharp short iron game should set you up for a birdie opportunity. As an advanced player, you should not only be able to land the ball on the smallest green, even with a seven-iron, but you should also be working the ball near the pin. Control and feel are the foundations for scoring with the short irons. Let me show you how.

The short irons - because of their shorter shafts - reduce the length of the swing. At address, you will have to stand close to the ball, or else you will not reach it with the clubhead without stretching your arms. Therefore, the angle of your swing will change from the sweeping blow to a steeper plane. This altered angle of your short iron swing leads to a more descending blow on the ball, imparting plenty of backspin to stop it dead near the cup.

As a consequence of the steeper swing plane, you should produce a sizeable divot if you hit your short irons correctly. You will remember that it is the angle of the swing that shapes the divot. The shorter the shaft, the steeper the swing plane, and the deeper the divot.

As the photographs on page 102 demonstrate, it is not even necessary to alter the ball position for the short irons. The short shaft allows you to hit the ball crisp and clean from its usual position opposite the left heel.

The Regular Short Iron Shot

Due to the shorter club shaft, you have to narrow your stance by two or three inches from your usual shoulder-wide set up position, and stand a little closer to the ball than you did for the mid irons. This posture will allow you to hit a short iron shot with precision and feel.

For maximum control over your shot, reduce your knee and hip rotation, both on the backswing and the follow through, and check your arm movement. You need to keep the arms close to your body, to fine-tune the exact distance of the shot you want to generate.

Although your knees stay comfortably flexed during the entire swing, your feet should be very still through impact for a very controlled and precise stroke. The weight transfer is minimal.

After a slow takeaway, your shoulders should rotate until they are almost perpendicular to the target line, both on the backswing and on the follow through. The hips stop to turn to the right before they have reached 30 degrees at the top of the swing.

The club is released by passing the right arm over the left rather than by uncocking the hands and straightening the wrists. After impact, the arms again stay tight to the chest for the complete follow through.

The Scoring Shots

The secret to working the short irons is spin. The mid iron approach as we have seen requires shaping the trajectory of the ball both in the air and on the ground. In principle, this applies also to the short irons. However, as we draw closer to the green, working the roll of the ball gains in importance.

Spin controls the trajectory of the ball in the air and, consequently, its path on the ground. The considerable loft of the short irons and the steeper, shorter swing they require impart more backspin on the ball than with other clubs.

Every ball needs backspin to fly. The more backspin it gets, the higher it usually flies. However, as we have discussed in the section on mid irons, a left-to-right spin - as for a fade, for instance - causes the ball to fly high as well, and to stop faster on the ground. By contrast, a drawspin causes the ball to fly low and to run longer on the ground, as does a ball with little backspin.

On the other hand, backspin exaggerates the curvature of the trajectory. Your fades and draws are more pronounced with a lot of backspin on the ball. Mistakes are aggravated. Little backspin has the opposite effect on the sidespin you shaped into the flight of your ball.

As a rule of thumb, backspin is imparted on the ball by a steep blow of a clubhead with a lofted club face at high speed. The steeper the blow, the more lofted the club, and the higher the clubhead speed, the more backspin is imparted on the ball.

To a lesser degree, backspin is affected by the material from which your clubhead is manufactured. Forged iron, for instance, allows the ball to stay a little longer on the club face than other materials through impact, and thus helps to generate more backspin. Another factor contributing to the backspin is your golf ball. For example, you will generate more backspin with a balata ball than with a two-piece Surlyn ball, because balata is a softer material that clings longer to the clubhead at impact. This difference in backspin between the types

OVERLEAF AND FOLLOWING PAGES: *The main difference between the short irons and the long and mid irons is the length of the swing. The club shafts are shorter so the arc of the swing is smaller. Stand a little closer to the ball with your feet two or three inches less than shoulder-width apart. Your arms should stay very tight to your chest, both on the backswing and the through swing to give you more control over the shot. My feet remain still as I rotate my lower body through impact. My hands stay passive, the club is released by the right arm crossing over the left arm, into a good, tight follow through.*

of balls is more pronounced with mid and long irons than with woods and wedges because the loft of the club face by far outweighs the other contributing factors.

The Approach with a Lot of Spin

You will need extra spin on your short iron ball if you have to land it on a very narrow green with a pin near a greenside bunker, for instance. The infamous par three eighth hole at Royal Troon with its postage-stamp-size green surrounded by weed-studded sand dunes and deep bunkers is a typical example of such a green.

Another dreaded approach shot is to a steeply inclined putting surface with a precarious flag position, regardless of whether the green slopes towards or away from you.

A word of warning before you try imparting more backspin on your short iron ball, though: the ball will always roll a little, and it certainly does not spin back once it lands past the flag as a carefully lobbed wedge shot might.

If you want to put extra backspin on your ball, stand a little closer to the ball than you usually would, perhaps by an inch or two, so that you can stand and swing in a more upright position. As a result the club face is delivered into the ball at a steeper angle, sending the ball off on a high trajectory with a lot of spin.

The Approach with Little Spin

To attack a green with several swales for instance, which run at an angle to you, your ball needs a little less spin and a better roll. The same applies if the green curves around a pond or another hazard and your angle of attack prevents you from aiming at the pin directly; or the pin is partially hidden behind shrubs.

When you need less spin on the ball for an uphill roll on the putting surface for instance, use your flat, wide swing plane with a three-quarter arc. Consequently, the club face strikes the ball at a shallower angle, resulting in less backspin.

Although the positions I just described resemble the set-up for the high and the low shots respectively, the trajectory of the ball and its backspin are two separate entities. As a matter of fact, you can put a lot of spin on low shots and little spin on high ones.

THE WEDGES

The nearer we come to the green, the more versatile shotmaking becomes. Wedges today are truly precision tools devised for a variety of purposes. I carry three of them in my bag. The obvious alternative to this is settling for three-quarter and half-swings with the pitching wedge. While none of these are difficult to execute, it can be a daunting task to estimate the exact length of your swing arc in order to reach, but not surpass your target. I believe three wedges give that extra edge which your opponents can only beat through hitting extremely accurate chips and pitches. As you fine-tune your skills, it makes sense to make use of the vast variety of equipment available to make your task easier.

The Use of Different Wedges

My normal pitching wedge has a rather steep loft of 49 degrees and serves me well at quite a distance from the green. The loft is enough to let the ball land gently or have it spin backwards if need be, while giving me reasonable distance, about 125 yards.

You should also carry a 'gap wedge'. Mine has a loft of 56 degrees, which serves me frequently on and off the fairways. A full swing with this wedge gives me a length between the reach of my pitching wedge, and the scope of my sand wedge. It makes a superb weapon for lob shots of the fringe.

The sand wedge, with a loft of 60 degrees, is most useful in bunker play because of its bounce. It is the only club in my bag that doesn't have an extra-stiff shaft so that I can finesse bunker shots better.

The Feel

The ability to hit a lot of different wedge shots, to spin the ball and to change the trajectory of the ball requires practice and feel, which depend predominantly on your club. Generally speaking, a heavy swing weight, that is a heavy clubhead in relation to shaft and grip, gives golfers a better feel than a light swing weight. For instance, I use a D 4 swing weight on my clubs, but, of course, I also have the strength to swing them. The swing weight of your clubs must be heavy enough to let you feel the club and light enough to let you generate reasonable clubhead speed.

LEFT: *The three wedges I carry from top to bottom: The pitching wedge, with a 49 degree loft, which I use mainly on the fairway at about 100 yards to the pin. The second wedge has 56 degrees loft, and is an ideal weapon from the fringe and out of tall grass around the green. The sand wedge, with 60 degrees loft, is designed for bunker use and not suitable for shots from the rough because of its flange.*

BELOW LEFT: *The set-up
positions for the full and the
three-quarter wedge shots
are the same.* OPPOSITE,
FAR LEFT: *At the top of the
backswing, restrict your hip
and shoulder turn well
before the shoulders are
perpendicular to the target
line.* LEFT: *The three-
quarter wedge shot is based
on less knee and hip
rotation.* THIS PAGE,
ABOVE LEFT: *The
centrifugal force created by
the clubhead speed through
impact carries you to a
rather complete follow
through of the full wedge
shot.* ABOVE: *The follow
through of the three-quarter
wedge is not far behind the
full swing in length.*

OPPOSITE, FAR LEFT, CENTER LEFT AND LEFT: *To create a low spinning wedge shot, the hands are set ahead of the ball at address, and the weight is concentrated on the left side. I keep the club low on the backswing and low on the through swing with my wrists cocked. This shallow approach to the impact zone keeps the flight of the ball down.*

OPPOSITE, FAR LEFT, CENTER LEFT AND LEFT: *The ball has again moved up in my stance for the high wedge. The weight remains predominantly on the right foot and the follow through is carried slightly higher than that of the low, spinning wedge. Through impact, there is no visible difference between these two shots.*

Feel, of course, lies in your hands, as they are the only contact you actually have with the club. The way you grip the club determines not only the way the club behaves, but also the feedback you receive from the clubhead during your swing. The harder you press on your grip, the less you will feel the clubhead; the lighter your grip pressure, the less control you will have over the club.

Your grip pressure should remain constant throughout your swing and throughout your game to add consistency to your swing. However, there are a few exceptions to this rule. You should use a firmer grip for shots out of a bad lie in the rough or a buried lie in the bunker to exercise more control over those.

A lighter pressure, on the other hand, allows you to pass your right hand over your left on the follow through of the flop chip and certain sand shots. It also gives you the feel and touch necessary for the delicate half- and three-quarter swings with wedges. So, lighten your grip for the wedge shots.

The Half Swing

It is an invaluable asset to know the exact distances of all your wedges on full swings, three-quarter swings and half swings and any swings you want to try in between. There is no shortcut to practicing; if need be you must pace the distances you generated. Once you have acquired this information, you will no longer be tempted to quit on your short wedge swings for fear of blasting the ball past the target.

The full swing, the three-quarter swing and the half swing differ only in the length of the swing arc. To hit any of these wedge shots, place the ball in the center of your stance, which is three or four inches narrower than your shoulder-width. Move slightly closer to the ball with your knees somewhat less flexed than for the short irons. The more upright stance allows you to deliver the clubhead crisply to the ball at a steep angle.

Open your stance slightly by pulling the left foot back by an inch or two behind the target line and open the club face in proportion to your stance so that you don't put sidespin on the ball. This address position will lead to a slightly steeper backswing, meaning you will hit the ball more precisely and impart a lot of backspin on it. Hold your grip lighter than you normally would.

On the backswing and the follow through, your knee, hip and shoulder rotation must be tightly controlled. Don't allow your shoulders to turn until they are perpendicular to the target line. An angle of 70 or 80 degrees instead is sufficient at the top of the swing.

It is at the top of the swing that you require feel most. The length of your backswing determines the length of the shot, and, as you can see on the photographs overleaf, the difference between a full and a three-quarter wedge shot is minute. Your hands should not be carried far above your shoulders, even for a full shot, which is hardly longer than the three-quarter shot. A half swing can be anything from a waist-high position of your hands to a three-quarter backswing. It is a matter of practice and feel to control the length of the wedge shots.

About 50 percent of your weight remains on your left leg throughout the swing so that you can accelerate firmly through impact and ensure a high trajectory of your wedge shot. Wedge shots are 'wristy' shots. While you should keep your hands passive during the longer game, as it will help you to control the club better, active hands are needed for the pitches, the wedges, and the bunker shots. You need a distinct hand release through impact and the feel to do it right.

The Low, Spinning Wedge

The low, spinning wedge is again almost a contradiction in terms: the low trajectory means low backspin, while high backspin means a high trajectory. It is crucial on this difficult shot to make very subtle adjustments to your set-up.

To achieve the low line of flight, move the ball back barely past the center between your feet. Shorten your swing according to the distance you want to reach, but keep it decidedly flat to shape the intended trajectory. The weight is predominantly on the left. Due to the very minute alteration of the ball position, your head is almost in line with the ball, but your hands are well ahead of it at address to impart the spin.

The High Wedge with Little Spin

This shot like the low, spinning wedge demands skill and finesse. The shot requires several adjustments to your swing since the high ball usually carries a lot of backspin. To set up, move the ball forward in your stance so that it comes to lie just an inch left of your left heel. This stance in effect moves head and hands behind the ball at address, allowing your hands to release early and to keep the club face squared to the target through impact.

The weight remains predominantly on your right foot to ensure the high trajectory of the ball. The key to this shot is a very slow swing through impact to reduce the backspin on the ball.

115

THE PUTTER

One of the most frustrating aspects of putting is the fact that the green suffers from play during the day. It's much easier to hole a putt in the morning before other golfers and their caddies have been walking around the hole, aligning their putts, marking their balls and tending their flags. Scientists have proven that one single flight of golfers leaves as many as several hundred footprints on the green, from which the grass doesn't recover for hours. The more players on the course, the worse it gets.

The footprints leave depressions in the green surrounding the hole at a six-foot radius, throwing your perfectly aligned putt off the track just as it slows down near the pin. What is worse, the area within a 12-inch radius of the cup doesn't get trampled on and warps due to all those depressions around it. In other words, after bumping around the footprints and knocking over ball and spike marks, the ball has to climb at the end of its roll. It is a small wonder, then, that even PGA Tour players miss 70 per cent of the 12-foot putts. With all these setbacks, you need a very consistent putting stroke and a sound strategy to sink your putts.

Putts fare better on well maintained greens. A test was conducted with the help of a putting machine on different US courses at a 12-foot distance to the cup. The machine managed to hole the putts in 50 percent of the cases on the average course and in 84 percent of the attempts on the well manicured course.

What throws a ball off balance in the last few yards? Unrepaired ball marks, and, ironically, repaired ones as well. When a ball leaves its imprint on the green, it pushes the soil and turf surrounding the depression to the side. To accommodate the ball, soil and turf warp, forming a little scar. Unless you repair the ball mark and the scar around it immediately, the scar remains.

Spike marks may also be the culprit when you miss your putts. Although many exclusive clubs prohibit players from wearing shoes with rubber soles and dimples, it has been asserted that the metal spikes are actually damaging the greens more. Where the rubber dimple merely presses the grass blade down for a couple of hours, the metal spike pierces and injures the root of the plant. And, of course, every time you make a step on the green, your spike isn't only dug in but also pulled out at an angle, throwing out a bit of soil - right into the line of someone's putt.

Shoes with soft spikes, which leave no marks on the greens, are currently being tested in several US golf clubs, with tremendous success. The introduction of soft spikes may present us with smoother putting surfaces in the future. But for the time being, most putts will bump along.

So, at the end of the day, your putt really doesn't stand much of a chance. All these little indents on the seemingly smooth putting surface loom large for a little white ball. So, putt early in the day, if you can. Putt firmly. A ball that is left short rarely makes it into the cup. And remember that all those little lumps, humps and holes in the line of your putt affect your ball more if it travels slowly.

The Pre-Putting Routine

To consistently strike my putts rhythmically and smoothly over and over again, I use the pre-swing routine illustrated on the following two pages. This routine sets my muscle-memory to work and fills me with the confidence to hole the putt - even under pressure. The identical movements precede all my putts, whether they are two- or 20-footers, whether they are played at Augusta or on my Florida practice green. You should do the same.

My pre-putt routine is not unlike the one I use to prepare for the other shots on the course. Again, I come up to the ball from behind with my putter in my right hand to check the line. I only crouch to take the bearings if this view does not give me any clues. You have probably seen me pick up the putter and hold the putter head in my left hand while I determine the line of putt.

In the photographs on page 118, you will also notice that I pick a spot on the green on my putting line, such a particular blade of grass, for my immediate target. I then ground the putter head square to the cup and align my feet parallel to the intended putting line. I double-check the line to the hole - and my immediate target - before I concentrate on striking the ball.

The Putting Grip

Some of the biggest problems on putting greens are uncontrolled wrist movements; in their worst form, they are known as 'the yips'. These are usually brought about by a fear of failure, and nothing but solid confidence in your putting stroke will save you from them. However, you can counteract uncontrolled wrist action in your putts even before you start developing problems by changing your grip.

Butch changed my putting grip, and worked wonders. My left hand was too much on top of the club and my right hand actually a little under the club. This

LEFT TO RIGHT, TOP TO
BOTTOM: *My pre-putting
routine, just like my usual
pre-swing routine, helps me
to focus my concentration on
the stroke I am going to
make and ensures
consistency in my game.
Here you can follow my
steps, which need not be
yours, from checking the
undulations of the green and
the grain, to determining the
line of my putt, choosing a
point in the grass to aim my
stroke at, feeling the weight
of the putter, aligning my
stance and double-checking
the putting line. Whatever it
is you do, always stick to
your routine, and you will be
rewarded.*

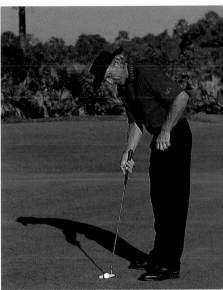

grip engaged the wrists too much, and it made me lift the putter head so high during the stroke that it prevented a smooth, even stroke.

I now putt with the forefinger of my left hand overlapping my right ring finger, and both the left and the right hand placed more under the shaft, opposite each other. My hands are straight in line with the ball to give me better control. The forefinger of my right hand is lying further down the shaft than the other fingers to give me more feel for my putting stroke.

The Putting Stroke

At address, I close my stance by moving my left foot about an inch closer to the target line to restrict my follow through. My weight is concentrated on the left foot at address, with somewhat more weight in the balls of my feet to keep me balanced. The ball lies in its usual position just opposite my left heel as for any other swing. I have a distinct tilt in my waist and a nice flex in my knees, and I don't stand up nearly as tall anymore as I used to. My eyes are almost directly over the ball so that I can view my line of putt with as few distortions as possible.

This posture allows me to let my arms hang down naturally with the elbows close to the body throughout the putt. As in my full swing, my putting stroke is a joint movement of the shoulders, arms and wrists together, from a little inside the straight putting line on the backswing to inside on the follow through.

I bend my wrists and elbows slightly to get a better feel of the putting stroke in my hands. You can see in the photographs on page 124 that the impact position is like the address position. I don't break my wrists, and the putter head is released through the ball at impact. This is something I used to practice by putting with my right hand only. Another problem area that I have worked on a lot is my head position. I make sure that I stay really still over the ball and watch the putter hit it. After impact, I follow through just as long and as high as I swung back.

The Different Putter Types

Putting is a very personal affair. The putter you chose should suit your style and please your eye. Manufacturers today offer putters for every whim and fancy: offset putters to move your hands a fraction in front of the ball; center-shafted and heel-shafted putters; blades; perimeter-weighted putters; and mallets. In fact, there are putters of just about any shape and size, and made of any material, with any sort of loft and shaft you can dream of.

120

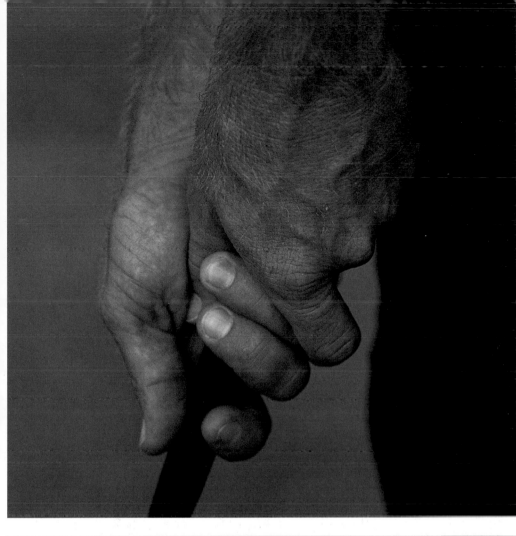

LEFT AND BELOW LEFT:
To gain more feel for my putts and to restrict my wrist action on the strokes, I have adopted a particular putting grip. You may want to try it if you find your existing one unbalanced, for instance if you tend to draw or fade all your putts around the hole instead of into it. My left forefinger overlaps the ring finger of the right hand, and both hands are placed under the shaft, rather than on it. You will notice that the forefinger of my right hand is lying further down the shaft than the other fingers, giving me a bit more feel for my putting stroke. I find that this grip allows me to move both my hands together while restricting unwanted wrist action.

THE PUTTING STROKE

RIGHT: *As you can see, my stance is quite close to the ball, with my elbows tight to the body and my eyes almost directly over the ball when I putt, so that I can see my putting line without any distortions. The putter blade actually swings back a little inside on the backswing and on the longer through swing. The putting stroke is not exactly straight.*

PRECEDING PAGES: *I strike the putt off my left heel like almost any other golf shot. This position is an ingrained part of my swing and allows me to carry some of the consistency from my long game over to the putting green. I also use part of my regular swing as my putting stroke for much the same reason. My weight is concentrated more on my left side at address to move the center of gravity - and the bottom of my swing arc - closer to the ball. The putter swings back and through, at an even pace. Notice how the left wrist does not break down at impact. The address position and the impact position are the same.*

Putters have a loft between zero and nine degrees to lift the ball up slightly, before it begins to roll. Without loft, putters would send the ball skidding across the green, and you would have a hard time trying to hole out. A higher loft is, of course, of use on longer grass and for the Texas wedge; and it may be a liability on a very smooth putting surface. Your home course conditions should be your guidance.

However, if you putt with your hands ahead of the ball, with a higher backswing than through swing, you will also benefit from a higher loft. It will prevent the ball from being pressed into the ground.

The reverse is true if you have your hands behind the ball when you putt. You need less loft on your putter, because you tend to catch the ball on the upswing, where a high loft would send it flying.

How far or how near you stand to the ball, will determine the lie of the ideal putter for you. The lie — the angle at which the shaft meets the clubhead — varies on putters from 66 to 79 degrees. If you prefer to stand close to the ball, with your eyes almost over it like I do, you will need a more upright lie than someone who stands farther from the ball with an inside-out stroke.

My preference has always been for a putter with the shaft near the heel. Although I have tried the center-shafted Bull's Eye blade at various times, I have always come back to my perimeter-weighted putter in the end. It gives me a better feel for the stroke, with its shaft close to the heel.

The Putting Strategy

Greens can be complex. If one detail is missing in the analysis, the carefully planned putt may end up a long way from the hole. Tiny dents, humps, ridges, slopes and swales in the green may be difficult to interpret, and other information about the soil and climatic conditions may not be readily available.

As a rule of thumb, smaller greens are less contoured than larger ones. Before checking the individual contours, the humps and mounds built into each green by the designer, consider the overall terrain surrounding the hole. Mountain greens tend to follow the natural terrain, while lake-side greens tend to drop towards the water. The fairway leading to the green may give you further information about the geographic conditions. Is the fairway rising towards the green or is it dropping near the hole? Does the green slope towards or away from you, or does it fall off sideways?

Designers usually have their idiosyncrasies about creating the greens: some prefer large, circular greens; some plan amoebae-shaped areas with uneven borders made of bunkers, shrubs or banks; others design tiny surfaces or multi-tiered greens. It helps to know your designer's preferences when playing a course for the first time. You are also well advised to keep the greenkeeper's priorities in mind. Designers frequently assist in the maintenance of the course by contouring the greens to fall away around the edges to drain water off the grass.

The underlying slant of the terrain is commonly the most pronounced contour in any green, and it is likely to most affect the line and speed of the putt. If the designer has built swales or tiers into the green, they will come into play next in line. For instance, once a ball crosses a ridge, it will roll down from it almost at a 90 degree angle to it, even if the ball arrived at the ridge at a totally different angle.

After having thus changed its course drastically, the ball will then adjust again quickly according to the overall slant of the green. In the meantime, the ball may have traveled on a huge semi-circle around the hole, leaving you with a long putt back to the cup. Having said that, if you are faced with a little three- or four-footer on a fast green with a subtle break, for example, you can hit the ball just a little harder and take that break out of it.

The speed of the putt on the green depends largely on the greenkeeper. If he cuts the grass high, your putt travels slowly; if he cuts it low, your putt travels fast. Right after the grass has been cut, the balls roll faster than on subsequent days. If the greenkeeper keeps the sprinkler running frequently, the greens lose speed. Bright green blades of grass offer greater resistance to your ball. If the grass is wet due to fog, rain or dew, it slows the putt, as does soggy soil; conversely, a warm afternoon sun or a persistent breeze may provide you with a dry, and hence, faster, putting surface.

A pronounced grain (the horizontal direction in which the grass grows) affects the speed of the putt and its line. Unfortunately, grain on the green rarely runs in one direction only. This may well be why less than 55 percent of the players on the PGA Tour sink their six-foot putts.

To check if the direction of the grain is with or against you is quite easy. When you look down at the green and the blades of the grass appear sunlit and shiny, the grain is with you. When the grass color looks dull, the grain is against you. There are, unfortunately, no shortcuts for checking the grain that crosses the line of your putt. You need to walk around the hole to find the direction of the grain, if discernible at all, before you can make allowances for sideways deviations.

You can also check the grain by examining the rims of the hole. Usually, one side of the cup appears somewhat frayed and not as beautifully cut as the other because the grass has been growing over the rim, following its grain. The terrain may also offer you a cue: the grain tends to grow away from mountains towards a body of water at the bottom. It is generally a good idea to make a couple of putts on the putting green before playing your round to familiarize yourself with the conditions of the greens.

Unfortunately, not all grass is equal. Bentgrass, for instance, grows vertically and therefore does not obstruct the putt with a distinct grain, while its fine leaves offer little resistance to the ball. Because it can be cut very low, Bentgrass makes for very fast putting surfaces. On the other hand, Fescue is a fine-bladed grass with wiry stems. It does not have much of a grain, but it slows your putt because of its bristly stalks and the high cut it requires. Bermudagrass has a broader blade, which can slow the putt, and a pronounced grain. It usually cannot be cut very low.

The Texas Wedge

The Texas Wedge is nothing more than putting from the fairway onto an open green. Obviously, you need to study the undulations on the fairway and the green, and the length of the grass you are playing on before you can use the putter on the fairway. If it has not been closely mown, the ball will stop dead on fringes, which a chip would easily jump across.

You see the Texas wedge in action frequently during the British Open Championships on golf courses in England, Ireland and Scotland whenever the pins are placed in the front of the greens or right up a slope, rendering a chip or a pitch extremely tricky.

Whenever you are stuck on a tight lie, the Texas wedge is especially helpful. The thick sole of a wedge easily bounces off a tight lie, resulting in extremely difficult pitches if you don't have enough grass under your ball.

Once you have decided on your strategy, just take your putter and set up as if for a putt. Be careful to keep your body still and your head down at impact, and treat the shot as if it was a long putt. The length of your backswing determines the distance the ball will roll. Sweep through the ball - not at it - and roll it onto the green. Don't forget to follow through, since you still have to accelerate through impact.

LEFT: *Using the putter off the green is a good idea when you face a difficult pitch, such as if the lie is not good or if there is not enough green to land the ball with a pitch shot. You need to treat the Texas wedge like a long putt. Keep your body still and your head down at impact. Sweep through the ball - not at it.*

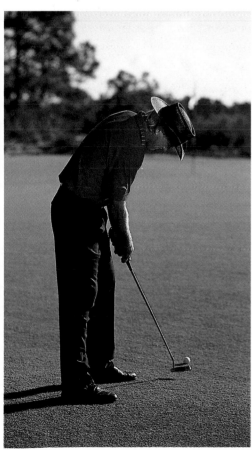

129

3. Shotmaking

THE CHIP SHOTS

Should you have missed your long approach shot to the green, as even competent professional golfers on the PGA Tour do 25 percent of the time, you have to demonstrate your chipping or pitching abilities to birdie or at least save par. Around the green, your shotmaking skills and technical expertise benefit you most. You always stand a chance to sink a ball from the fringe.

There must be hundreds of different possibilities to hole a ball from within the 100-yard range, including the punch shot and the Texas wedge described earlier. There are the high, soft-landing pitch shots which can travel any distance from over a hundred yards to two or three yards, according to the length of your backswing. Chip shots fly lower and run longer on the ground. They can be almost as flat as putts, barely skimming over the green, or reach the height of a short pitch shot and cover many yards in their roll.

The tricky little shots around the green require feel - for the clubhead - and touch - for the execution of the shot. To master the challenges of chipping and pitching, I recommend you to make three slight adjustments to your set-up. Most importantly, don't wear your gloves. All of these shots - with the exception of the full pitch - require finesse and a lot of feel in your fingertips which you cannot get with a glove.

In addition, grip down on the shaft. Choking down will reduce the arc further for greater control, even if you make a full swing. Without absolute control over the clubhead, your stroke won't be precise enough to drop a diminutive ball into a tiny cup from 20 yards off.

Last but not least, open your stance. Pull your left foot back by about an inch and open the left knee, hip and shoulder to the target. Don't forget to open the clubface as well to avoid putting sidespin on the ball. The open address position enables you to move the left side of your body out of the way quickly on the through swing. You can now also swing back and through on a slightly steeper angle, imparting more backspin on the ball. As a result, it will fly higher and stop earlier than it normally would.

On the following pages are detailed instructions for the short shots I commonly use, employing clubs as varied as a three-wood, a four-iron, an eight-iron, and a wedge. When practicing your chipping and pitching techniques on the range, don't restrict yourself to the short clubs only. Every single one of your clubs - including your long irons - has a distinct flight and roll pattern on chip and pitch shots. So, arm yourself with a notebook and a pen and jot down exactly how each club performs with your short game. This exercise will turn you into an expert shotmaker.

Before you decide on the club and the type of shot you want to play, ideally you should know the conditions on the green and prepare for the stroke just as you would for a putt. If you are playing on a course unknown to you, however, it is usually not possible to scout the green when your ball lies hundred yards in front of the putting surface.

Here again you stand to benefit from a few practice strokes on the putting green prior to your round. This will tell you how the greens out on the course are likely to react. Are they hard and bound to yield a lot of roll? Or will a high pitch result in a plugged ball? Is it safe to putt from the fringe or will the high grass on the apron stop your ball dead in its tracks? The weather, the time of day, the soil and the grass all affect your short shots as much as your putts.

Gather as much information as you can from other players or the greenkeeper. Watch your competitors. You can eliminate much of the guesswork from your strategy and really start planning your round.

The Pitch

The pitch is little more than a high, soft-landing shot with a lofted wedge; which club to chose depends on the distance you need to reach. At the end of the day, nobody will be impressed if you hit your wedge 135 yards and miss the green. Above all: don't take a short club and try to power the ball near the pin - this strategy fails every day on all golf courses around the world.

Due to the shorter club shaft, you have to narrow your stance by probably four inches from your usual shoulder-wide set-up position. The length of the club shaft has created a shorter swing arc, allowing you more control over the shot.

The photographs on page 134 document that I do stand at a fair distance to the ball with my knees more than usually flexed and the waist distinctly tilted. Most of the weight remains on my left leg throughout the pitch.

You need to stand firm through impact for an easy, fluent swing. Imagine you are hitting from the top of a butter cream cake, where any abrupt movement would send you slipping.

At address, open your stance slightly by pulling the left foot back by an inch or two behind the target line to open shoulders, hips and knees to the target. Of

THE REGULAR PITCH

For the regular pitch, you need to be aware exactly how long you hit each of your clubs at different lengths of your backswing to choose a club with the right loft for the shot. RIGHT: My stance is four inches narrower than shoulder-width. The knees, as you see, are flexed. The hip rotation is curtailed, and so is the shoulder turn. The weight transfer should be slight, and most of it remains on the left side throughout the stroke. You need to stay firm for a successful pitch shot.

134

course, you will also have to open the club face, so that you don't put sidespin on the ball. The open stance will lead to a slightly steeper backswing. As a consequence, you will hit the ball more precisely and impart a lot of backspin on it.

Grip down the shaft to get greater control over the club as your hands get closer to the clubhead and the ball. By moving your hands down the shaft, you have in effect shortened your swing arc further, even if you make a full swing.

Breaking your hands early on the backswing will keep the swing arc as steep as possible. The ball is thus picked up crisply through impact. During the shortened follow through, the wrists break again fairly soon after impact.

If you follow my example, you will impart a lot of backspin on your pitch shot. The ball will fly high, land softly, and roll very little - picture-perfect. Compare the photographs on pages 134 to 135.

The Regular Chip

The hands are the key to the various chip shots. While the ball position regulates the height of the trajectory - back in the stance for a low line of flight and forward in the stance for a high line of flight - the hands determine the relation between flight and roll of the ball. In other words: the hands provide the spin that can stop a low ball or spirit a high ball on a long roll.

For the regular chip, place your hands well in front of the ball, in line with your left thigh. Otherwise, the set-up is not very different from the pitch. The narrow stance and the ball position remain identical. Concentrate your weight slightly more on the right foot than during a normal swing. There is not much weight transfer in the chip shots, due to the rather short swing arc.

The chip comes closest to a pendulum movement of arms and shoulders without any engagement of the wrists. The clubhead stays low during take away and through swing. During the backswing and follow through the wrists barely bend and remain straight through impact. You see clearly the passive wrists with the back of the left hand actually leading the club head through impact in the top two photographs on page 137.

Since the forward hand position has, in effect, neutralized some of the loft of the club, the result of the chip is a short, low flight of the ball and a long roll. A seven-iron chip spends usually one third of the entire distance covered in the air and two thirds on the ground. With a pitch, the ball will fly half the way.

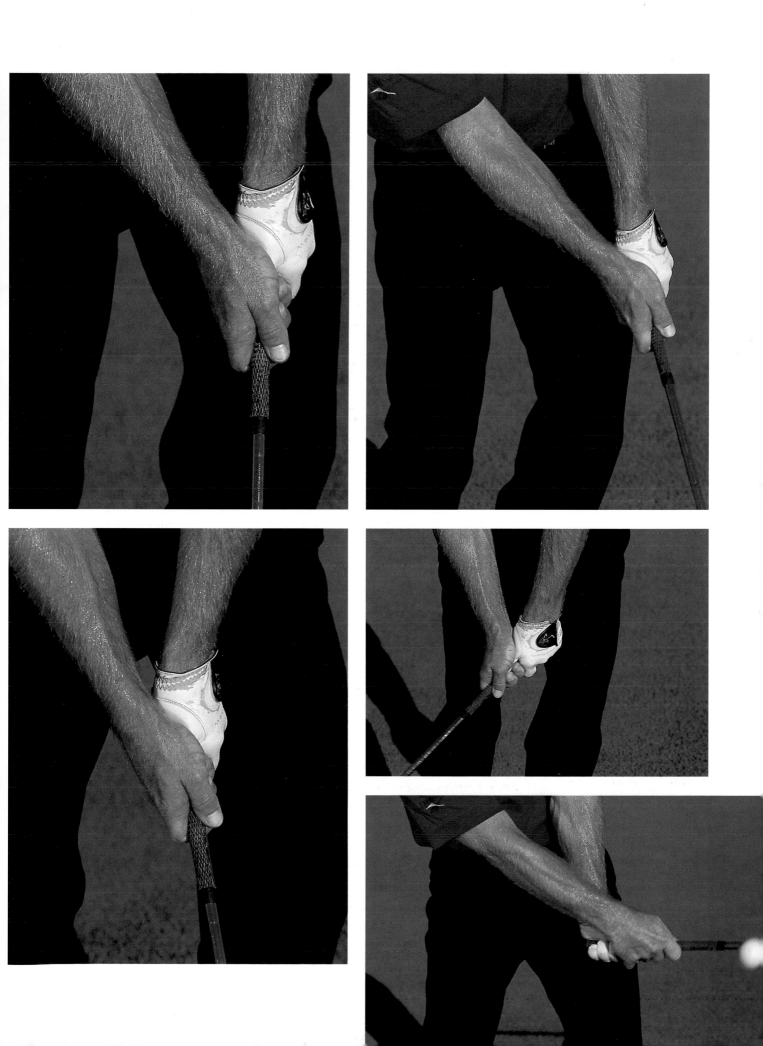

THE FLOP CHIP

PRECEDING PAGES, PAGE 138, TOP LEFT: *Open the club face at address.* TOP RIGHT: *Break the club at a steep angle on the backswing.* PAGE 139, TOP LEFT: *The flop chip in this case is carried to a three-quarter backswing, with a restricted shoulder turn of about 70 degrees right of the address position and a hip rotation of 35 degrees.* PAGE 138, BELOW LEFT: *Release the club early on the downswing, letting the clubhead pass your hands at impact. Stay down and let the loft of the club get the ball in the air.* BELOW RIGHT AND PAGE 139, BELOW LEFT: *The arms stay straight well past waist-high on the follow through. You can clearly see the crossing over of the hands. The finish shows a belt buckle square to the target and shoulders carried past perpendicular to the line of stroke.*

THE BLADED WEDGE

OPPOSITE: *When you can't get a putter between the fringe and the ball, use an open sand wedge like a putter for this specialty chip shot which I describe in detail on page 173.*

The Flop Chip

The flop chip for a super-soft lob is the direct opposite of the regular chip. It is the most 'wristy' of the chips with very little movement of arms and shoulders during the backswing and follow through.

From your regular set-up position, start with an open club face - for a higher trajectory - and the hands behind the ball to allow the clubhead to pass the hands through impact. This adds effectively to the loft of the club and results in a higher trajectory.

The photographs on page 137 illustrate the hand positions of the flop chip during address, takeaway and follow through compared to the regular chip. At address, you notice that my right hand is straight, while the left wrist is bent. The picture to the right shows the 'wristy' takeaway which causes a very steep backswing, adding extra height to the trajectory.

On top of the swing, your hips should have rotated 35 degrees to the right and your shoulders about 70 degrees on a three-quarter arc. Again, the length of the backswing determines the carry of your ball.

After the downswing, however, the arms and hands become active. The clubhead is released early in front of the hands, and the right hand rolls over the left through impact, guiding the left to the follow through. You have to take care to stay down on the shot and let the loft of the club get the ball airborne. Keep your arms straight well past waist-high on the follow through and take only the merest hint of a divot.

The Bump-And-Run Chip

The bump-and-run chip often looks like a mishap with the ball scrambling across the undulations on the green. Its initial trajectory is low and it is bound to bounce off firm greens several times before settling down to a long roll.

You need to know the humps and mounds in front of and on the putting surface before considering this option; bump-and-run balls have been known to take the most surprising turns on hidden swales. If you know your course well and are familiar with the way angles act on balls, you have a definite advantage over your competitors.

On the pages overleaf, I use an eight-iron for my bump-and-run chip, but the shot can be hit with all short irons. Just bear in mind that a ball hit with a shorter club will fly more and run less than one hit with a longer club.

140

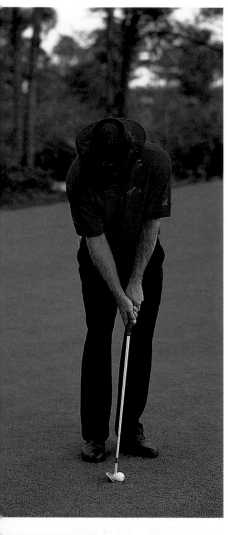

OPPOSITE, FAR LEFT: *The ball is positioned back, in a very narrow stance. The hands are ahead of the ball at address.* **BELOW FAR LEFT:** *The backswing is little more than a one-quarter arc and stops before the club has even reached parallel to the ground at the waist-high position.* **CENTER LEFT:** *The weight remains predominantly on the left side throughout the stroke, preventing the creation of much backspin which would result in a high trajectory. Little actual weight transfer takes place.* **LEFT:** *The hands lead the clubhead through impact, delofting the club and keeping the ball down.* **THIS PAGE:** *The follow through is a mirror-image of the backswing, determining the distance of the shot.*

THE FOUR-IRON CHIP

The four-iron chip ball will fly low and roll fast.
ABOUT: *The clubhead is hovering behind the ball.*
RIGHT: *On the backswing, the club reaches parallel to the ground on the waist-high position to allow the ball to cover the 50 yards between me and the pin.* OPPOSITE, RIGHT: *It is vital to accelerate through the ball at impact while the feet are firmly grounded and passive.* FAR RIGHT: *The follow through is as high as the backswing.*

144

Keep your feet very close together at address. The stance is slightly open, with your left foot still pointing outward and drawn back behind the target line by an inch. The knees remain well flexed and the waist is tiled. You also need to stand extremely close to the ball with your eyes literally over it.

To induce a low trajectory, you need to place the ball back in center of the stance. Keep your weight predominantly on the left foot and position your hands ahead of the ball. The takeaway is again very 'wristy', and the backswing is no longer than a one-quarter arc, as is the follow through. The hands lead the clubhead on the downswing while the wrists stay quiet through impact. This action will, in effect, deloft the club. The follow through determines the distance of your shot.

The Four-Iron Chip

The four-iron chip is the ideal weapon to attack a very long very long green. In the photographs on pages 144 and 145, you see me hitting this shot from about 50 yards to the pin. It would be very difficult, given the length and the undulations of the green, to hole the ball with a putter. Although I use a four-iron in the pictures, a three-iron is equally adequate. It will generate a similar line of flight with a longer roll.

To set up, I place the ball back in my stance, opposite my right heel. My backswing is higher than the one for the eight-iron bump-and-run chip with a bit more of a shoulder turn. The club reaches parallel to the ground in the waist-high position during the backswing.

My hands are ahead of the ball throughout the swing, and actually lead into this shot. It is vital to accelerate through the ball at impact, while the feet are firmly grounded and passive. There is very little wrist cock and the follow through stays low. The result is a very low-flying ball with a fast and long roll.

The Chipping Mistakes

The so-called 'flick wrist' - a collapse of the left hand at impact - is frequently encountered in the game of experienced golfers. If you scoop the ball through impact without solid contact, scrutinize your hand and wrist movements during your chip shots closely. You may discern the breaking of your left wrist on your through swing. For the flop chip, the right hand rolls over the left through impact, while the left wrist rotates to the left, but doesn't break. With a flip wrist, there is no rotation, only the break.

THE BUNKER SHOTS

Pot bunkers, sand dunes, fancy shapes and overhanging lips - golfers love to hate sand traps. Personally, though, I much prefer to get stuck in a bunker than in knee-deep rough, a puddle of water or under a tree. I have two good reasons for this. First, there are sand shots for just about any sort of situation and any type of sand a golf ball can get beached in. Practicing those shots will leave you well prepared out on the course brimming with confidence, because you know exactly how the sand will react and what kind of trajectory you will generate. Second, bunkers can be stroke-savers. The designers often place them where missing the sand could land you in deep trouble — out-of-bounds or in a pond, for instance.

On average, a course contains around a hundred bunkers. Some have up to two hundred, others are extremely difficult despite featuring only forty sand traps, like Augusta National does. As a rule of thumb, bunkers assist you in gauging distances. Hazards, especially on dog-leg holes, can even serve as a target for your shots, if you know that your shot will either be short or carry over it.

Your best bet before selecting a type of shot out of a bunker, is to walk into the trap to get a feel for the sand it contains, which usually stems from the surroundings of the course. River sands tend to be quite hard. They drain well, and you will rarely find a buried lie in them. Limestone sand - or coral if you play in the tropics - can be either fine or coarse, but both varieties are softer than river sand, letting your ball sink in deeper. The consolation is that they allow you to impart plenty of backspin on the ball. But beware if the sand you find your ball in is sparkling white and soft, as it is most likely silica sand, which tends to bury balls without allowing much backspin on them.

The Full Explosion

The full explosion is probably the easiest of the bunker shots. The club face does not hit the ball and a solid swing is all it takes to splash the ball out with the sand, landing it safely on the green. However, there are a couple of considerations in full explosion shots which tend to be overlooked. I have therefore provided a detailed examination of the full explosion shot. This will also help us to find the common ground from which to embark on the more elaborate bunker shots.

The full explosion shots - like most bunker shots - are played with an open club face. It is of immense importance to take the club in your right hand and open it

148

before you take the grip. If you take your grip first and then open the club face, it will return to the position you started, square to the target, when the club face hits the sand.

Obviously, you now also have to open your stance, since the open club face would be aiming way out to the right of the target if you were standing parallel to the intended line of flight. Dig your feet into the sand so that the ball rests opposite the left heel with your left foot, knee and hip open to the left of the target. Your stance should be fairly wide so that you stand firmly and comfortably in the sand with the knees well flexed.

The neck of the sand wedge is pointed down the intended line of the stroke. Since it is less deflected from the target line by the sand than the rest of the clubhead, you should aim and hit the ball more with the hosel of the club. I play my bunker shots with the ball opposite my left heel so that the bottom of the swing arc is where the club hits the sand - two or three inches behind the ball.

The main difference between the full explosion and a regular wedge shot lies in the angle of the swing arc. For the full explosion, I start to cock my wrist very early in the backswing, creating a very steep angle in the takeaway. The club is carried more around the body than over it, on top of the backswing, by cocking the wrists.

My shoulders turn just a little depending on the length of the backswing. The steep swing arc allows my right hand to slap the wedge into the sand, with the right hand about two to three inches behind the ball through impact. The sole of the wedge will bounce through the sand, not dig into it, throwing sand and ball out of the hazard. The speed of the clubhead through impact determines the distance the ball will carry. The club travels no further than parallel to the target line on the follow through.

The Soft Explosion

For the soft explosion, a shot that requires finesse and touch, quite a number of adjustments have to be made to the normal swing. To get the right feeling for the use of your wrists and hands, lighten the pressure on your grip and hold the club not nearly as firmly as you normally do. Open your club first, then take your grip and open your stance. Focus your eyes on a spot about two inches behind the ball where the club is going to enter the sand. Don't look at the ball which is placed forward in the stance.

The soft explosion is, of course, a high shot with almost no roll at all. If I am very close to the pin, I actually position my hands back behind the club face to

OVERLEAF AND FOLLOWING PAGES: *For the full explosion shot in the bunker, you must cock your wrists at a very steep angle on the backswing to return the club with a directly descending blow to the sand. The wrists and hands, especially on the right side, are very active in this shot. If you look closely at the position of my right hand in the following six photographs, you will see that the back of my right hand is basically rotating through impact, throwing the sand and the ball out of the bunker. You regulate the distance the ball travels through the speed and the length of the follow through.*

149

The full explosion requires a wide stance to settle firmly in the sand. OPPOSITE, RIGHT: The ball is placed off the left heel and the club face is opened, pointing almost 40 degrees to the right of the target line. FAR RIGHT: Wrist cocking early on the takeaway ensures a steep swing arc. BELOW RIGHT: The club is carried more around the body than over it, on top of the backswing, by cocking the wrists. Hip and shoulder turns are restricted. BELOW FAR RIGHT: The club is carried no further than parallel to the target line on the follow through.

get the ball up in the air faster. With the club face ahead of my hands, the shaft points almost back towards my right hip. This set-up presets my impact position and gives me the feeling of sliding the club underneath the ball through impact, to get the ball straight up and straight down. The ball doesn't get much spin and it doesn't roll very much.

The soft explosion is played on a very steep swing plane to control the amount of sand the clubhead digs through and, thus, the distance the ball travels. On the backswing, you should ensure that your left wrist gets into a weak or cupped position slightly more on top of the club. If it stayed straight, the club face would be squared through impact; you wouldn't be able to utilize the balance on the golf club when the right hand slaps the sand with the flange of the golf club through impact. Again, the speed of the shot and the length of the backswing determine the distance the ball will fly.

The Nip Chip

Nipping a ball, hitting it crisp and clean off the sand, is an unusual bunker shot. I may play a nip chip on wet sand out of a fairway bunker perhaps 30 or 40 yards from the pin, provided the hazard is flat and sports no overhanging lip. Whilst the regular bunker shot demands that you hit two or three inches behind the ball, the nip chip requires contact.

To set up for the nip chip - as for the other low trajectory shots - align the ball an inch or so inside the left heel. The length of the swing arc, both before and after impact, depends on the distance you need to generate, but the swing of this chip will typically not surpass a three-quarter arc.

Flatten the angle so that the swing remains wide during the backswing and follow through. This generates enough clubhead speed at impact for the ball to reach the pin, while providing a low trajectory at the same time. The ball leaves the loft of the club face through impact at a right angle. Due to the ball position, the loft of the wedge is effectively reduced through the impact zone which lies before the bottom of the swing arc is reached. In other words: depending on the length of the swing arc, the nip chip will propel the ball much farther than a normal wedge shot would.

However, on a bunker shot, the club face must not be delofted too much or it will not bounce through the sand after impact. Instead, it will dig in, and ruin the distance of your shot by preventing a proper follow through.

For the nip chip out of a bunker, your hands are therefore aligned right on top of the ball at address and retain this position throughout the swing. In this way,

156

the loft of the wedge will remain high enough through impact to impart as much backspin on the ball as is needed to stop it quickly on the green.

Seve's Eight-Iron Bunker Shot

My great Spanish colleague Severiano Ballesteros is a legendary trouble-shooter on the golf course. He is also one the most creative trap players I know. I was - and still am - particularly impressed with the eight-iron explosion shot which I learned from him and which has since become an integral part of my game. Very few professionals use this shot since it requires more finesse, skill and touch than any other.

Seve's eight-iron explosion shot works best from a distance of 30, 40 or even 50 yards to the green. As for most bunker shots, opening the club face prevents the eight-iron from digging too deeply into the sand. When you dig your feet into the sand so that the ball rests opposite the left heel, ensure that the left side of your body is open to the left of the target. Again, your stance should be fairly wide so that you stand firmly and comfortably in the sand, with the knees well flexed. The neck of the eight-iron is pointed down the intended line of your stroke.

Cock your wrist early in the backswing to cause a steep angle in the takeaway and downswing, as for the full explosion wedge shot. The length of the backswing and through swing determine - in conjunction with the clubhead speed - the carry of the shot, and your shoulders should turn accordingly. Let your right hand lead the eight-iron into the sand through impact about two inches behind the ball.

As a result of the loft of the clubhead and the length of the shaft of the eight iron, you generate a higher clubhead speed through impact, the ball emerges much faster from the sand, and travels at a much lower trajectory than on a regular explosion shot. The ball subsequently flies further and rolls a little on the green.

The Fairway Bunker Shot

To hit the ball a fair distance out of a bunker, the clubhead must strike the ball first and the sand second. To ensure this sequence of events, I stand up taller to the ball than I usually would for a trap shot so that I can sweep the ball clean off the sand. The set-up is similar to the address of the shot from a hardpan lie.

My stance is open, but rather narrow, so that I swing smoothly without using too much leg drive on the less than solid sand foundation. For the same reason,

OPPOSITE, FAR LEFT: *Once you have taken your slightly narrower stance for the soft explosion, open the club face first, then take your grip. Offset the fact that the club face is open by opening your stance.* CENTER LEFT AND LEFT: *The backswing must be very steep. Cock the wrist up quickly on the backswing.* BELOW CENTER LEFT: *You will slap the sand with your right hand, sliding the club under the ball in the sand.* BELOW LEFT: *You do not need much follow through on this shot.*

RIGHT AND OPPOSITE:
*The soft explosion is played
with an even steeper angle of
the swing arc than the full
explosion to control the
amount of sand the clubhead
digs through and, thus, the
distance the ball travels.
Notice the flex in my knees
despite my narrow stance.
Although the weight transfer
on the soft explosion is
slight, the flexed knees work
much like the suspension of a
car and keep me well
balanced through the sandy
impact.*

OPPOSITE AND OVERLEAF: *This shot differs drastically from the explosion shot in that you want to hit the ball first - not the sand. To ensure that you do so, stand a little taller. You can see clearly in the photographs on the following pages that my knees are much less flexed, and my waist less tilted than for the regular bunker shot, so that I can sweep the ball off the sand. Since the sand offers poor footing at best, you cannot use your legs to drive through the impact zone.*

I use a nine-iron for a 130-yard bunker shot in the photographs on page 165. This is a longer club than I would employ for the same distance off the fairway, allowing me to swing easily and keep my balance in spite of the poor footing. On the backswing, I cock the club up at a steeper angle to catch the ball just as crisply on the down and through swings. The follow through actually throws ball and sand out of the bunker and therefore has to be rather longer than for other bunker shots.

The Buried Lie

A buried bunker ball is a frequent enough occurrence, although rarely a reason for celebration. The remedies proposed vary from a closed to an open club face; there is a time and a place for either option. If played with a closed club face, the ball will travel on a lower trajectory and roll longer on the green. It may also get stuck on a high bunker wall.

Personally, I like to play this shot with a very open club face. If you want to be sure to get the ball up and out in one, set up just as you did for the soft explosion, with an open, fairly wide stance. However, the ball is now placed in the center between your feet. Since the ball is buried, you must catch it at the bottom of the swing arc to pop it out. Concentrate your weight on your left side and align the hosel of the club to the intended line of flight.

Hold the club a little tighter in your grip. This shot demands plenty of feel in the wrists and hands to prevent them from propelling the ball past the green since it will roll a lot. It also requires a very firm hit into the sand although the right hand does not pass under the left at impact on this shot; it is struck through impact, rather like a chip, with straight wrists.

Pick the club up sharply at the takeaway. The backswing is really a half arc on a very steep angle, allowing for an equally sharp and fast downswing. At the top of the swing, the hands are carried about shoulder-high. Stay down with straight hands and arms through impact. As you cock the club up and stick it down in the ground behind the ball, it pops the sand and the ball up. Since the ball was buried in the sand, there is hardly any backspin imparted on it through impact, resulting in a long roll on the green. There is absolutely no follow through on this shot.

The Shot From Wet Sand

Wet sand is firmer than dry sand and the ball will come out faster from it. Therefore, you need to adjust the speed of your swing to avoid hitting the ball

162

past the green. The correct timing of your swing can only be discovered with practice. Wet sand also poses another problem: if the sand is very hard, the sole of the sand wedge may let the club bounce off the sand. So, occasionally, you have to use your pitching wedge for the explosion shot in wet sand.

The shot from wet sand is another full explosion shot, and as such, it is played with an open club face and an open stance. Dig your feet into the sand so that the ball rests opposite the left heel with your left foot, knee and hip aimed to the left of the target. Grip down on the shaft for a better feel. The neck of the club is pointed down the intended line of my stroke.

For the explosion from wet sand, cock your wrist early on the takeaway to create a steep swing arc. The reduced shoulder turn keeps the speed of the clubhead under control. The steep swing arc allows your right hand to slap the wedge into sand through impact about two to three inches behind the ball.

The Uphill Lie

Slopes, whether in bunkers or out on the fairways, require an alignment of the shoulders so that they remain parallel to the ground. On an uphill lie, the left shoulder moves up, and the right shoulder down; on a downhill lie, the reverse applies. The purpose of this adjustment is to keep the vertical axis of the swing arc (from top to bottom) at a right angle to the ground, preventing the clubhead from getting stuck in the slope.

In the photographs on pages 170 and 171, note that I set up with an extremely wide stance for the shots from a bunker slope. Not only are the slopes quite severe, necessitating a more solid foundation for the swing; the sand is also rather fluffy at the Medalist Club, providing an even less stable foundation for the swing. Only a very wide stance puts me on a reasonable footing under the circumstances. The weight is concentrated on the right foot to provide a good balance throughout the swing.

I dig my feet into the sand so that the ball lies in the center between my feet. As my shoulders are already aligned parallel to the ground and the swing arc thus at a right angle to it, the ball position ensures that I capture the ball at the bottom of the swing arc.

My hands appear to be in line with the ball at address on the uphill lie, but since the vertical axis of the swing arc meets the ground at a right angle, my hands are actually in front of the ball in relation to the axis. If my hands were indeed in line with the ball, the swing axis would cause the ball to pop straight up and down without covering any distance on the uphill slope. The uphill lie still results in a very high trajectory, necessary to carry the slope in front - and I have to hit the sand hard to get the distance I want. This is because the clubhead on an uphill lie travels through more sand than during a straight bunker shot since the terrain is rising in front of the player.

I align the hosel of the club right on target, while my stance and the club face are more than usually open. The swing resembles a full explosion shot, with an early wrist cock on the takeaway and a steep angle of the swing. Again, it is the right hand which slaps the wedge into sand through impact about two to three inches behind the ball. The desired length of the shot is regulated by the speed of the clubhead through impact and the length of backswing and follow through.

The Downhill Lie

The downhill lie requires an even wider stance for proper balance during the shot since gravity is pulling the player down the slope. With my shoulders aligned parallel to the slope, the right below the left, the weight is now concentrated on the left side. In taking up my stance, the ball is positioned a little back in my stance. Since the vertical axis of the swing arc is now at a right angle to the downhill slope, the ball would hardly be skimming the ground if it was positioned straight in the center.

The key on the downhill shot is the cocking of the left wrist into a weak position. If you have a close look at the following photographs, you will detect that my left hand is shaped as if it held a little cup in it. The swing resembles a chip shot, with active wrists, but very little shoulder turn or weight transfer. The feet remain still through impact.

I cock the club straight up on the back swing and slap the sand with the clubhead approximately two inches behind the ball at impact to pop the ball out of the bunker. The cocking of the wrist restricts the swing arc and gives me more control over the clubhead speed at impact.

On the downhill slope, the ball emerges from the sand fairly quickly because there remains very little sand to deal with through impact as the terrain falls away from the golfer. Consequently, I don't have to hit the sand as hard as on an uphill slope. For the very short shot from the greenside bunker documented in the photographs on the following pages, I also don't need much of a follow through. I have allowed for these circumstances by cocking the club straight up on the back swing, restricting swing arc, clubhead speed and follow through and sending the ball straight to the green.

THE BURIED LIE

TOP: *This is a typical buried lie, with only half the ball exposed in wet sand. The club face is open to the target by about 45 degrees and the shaft is aligned to the target.* ABOVE: *This is the buried lie prior to impact, with the clubhead traveling through the sand.*

THE BURIED LIE

RIGHT: *The ball is placed in the center of your stance, which is wide - to give your swing a good foundation since you have to hit the sand very hard - and open - to offset the open club face at address.* FAR RIGHT: *Pick the club up very sharply on the backswing to allow the clubhead to hit the sand at an equally steep angle. The clubhead has to dig into the sand deeper than the buried ball. At the top of the swing, the hands are carried just about shoulder-high.* BELOW RIGHT: *The open club face, which meets the sand behind the ball, and the steep angle of approach pop the ball straight up.* OPPOSITE: *Stay down with straight hands and arms through impact. Remember also not to use a follow through. Because of the amount of sand the clubhead had to travel through in the buried lie, your ball will have no spin on it, so it will run when it comes out of the bunker.*

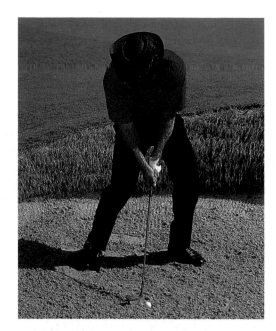

168

Remember to set your shoulders parallel to the angle of the slope. Your vertical swing axis will then be perpendicular to the slope that your ball is on. On the uphill slope, you must swing up the slope. RIGHT: Set up with a wide stance to balance your swing, with the weight concentrated on the right foot.

170

On the downhill slope, you must swing down the slope. FAR LEFT: *Use a wide stance for balance, with the ball a little back in the stance and the weight on the left foot.* LEFT: *The swing is almost like a chip shot, with active wrists but very little shoulder turn or weight transfer.* BELOW FAR LEFT: *The feet are again quiet through impact, while the clubhead strikes the sand behind the ball and travels quite a distance through it.* BELOW LEFT: *The trajectory is very shallow. You need to stay clear of any high obstacles with this shot. Playing it safely out at an angle to the pin may be your only option if faced with a huge bunker lip.*

171

THE TROUBLE SHOTS

The ideal of a good golfer is, of course, to stay out of trouble. However, if you have watched the world's top professionals during major tournaments on both sides of the Atlantic, you have seen quite a number of them in deep trouble time and again. There is no reason to believe that the advanced amateur fares any better than they do. This is why I have included in this book a number of shots I use on the rare occasions that my ball disappears in the bushes, and I can't employ one of my more common shots.

Trouble shooting demands a precise analysis of the situation. You need to assess the feasibility of possible escape shots. Rely on the strength of your swing, on strokes which you play well. If you haven't practiced a shot, don't attempt to hit it. You need to know your strengths and weaknesses and use this knowledge to your advantage to get out of trouble.

When your ball hugs the root of a tree or takes a mud bath in a swamp, a vivid imagination and some original thinking come at a premium. I regularly use creative mental-imaging techniques. They are in fact part of my pre-shot routine because they help me to activate my muscle memory. Visualization is even more essential when your ball skips the fairway and scuttles into the shrubs instead.

Visualize the shot that you are going to play every time you swing, like I do. If you use your imagination in the rough, you will discover for yourself which shots may not get you back to the fairway and onto the green. But you will also see the shot that will.

Imagine hitting a perfect shot; hear the club face hit the ball; and see the ball flying through the opening between the trees, underneath the branches; watch it land and roll towards the pin. Then swing. The picture you created in your mind will trigger your muscle memory and let you hit the ball out of trouble.

The Right-Handed Shot

Hitting the ball single-handed - with the right hand, if you are a right-hander like me - is an ideal shot for pitching the ball back out to the fairway when it sits snug against the wrong side of a tree trunk or some other immovable obstruction. Controlling the path of the clubhead and its speed with only one hand requires a lot of practice. Therefore, the single-handed shot should not be attempted for the first time out on the golf course. I never hit single-handed with the left hand; it's better suited for left-handers as they can muster much more control over the shot in that hand than I can.

As a single-handed shot is hit with the back to the target, you need to make sure you have the maximum control over the shot under the circumstances. Therefore, use for this shot an eight- or a nine-iron, and choke down the shaft with your right arm fully extended. It is very important to let your arm hang down straight to avoid topping the ball or missing it altogether.

The reason for this is simple: the club face, even when squared to the target offers only a fraction of its usual surface to the ball through impact because the leading edge of the club can never be parallel to the ground in this position. It is difficult to square the club face to the target to begin with since you cannot see the pin from your address position.

Set up for this stroke in a very tall position, with a narrow stance in which your feet are aligned at a right angle to the target. Place the ball almost in line with your feet, a little in front of them and about as far from your right foot as your left foot is from your right. This position ensures that your body does not obstruct your swing.

The stroke itself resembles a pendulum-movement: take the club straight up going back, hit the ball and go straight through without any out-to-in or in-to-out swinging of the club. The wrist releases through impact to propel the ball out of trouble.

The Bladed Wedge

The sand wedges are versatile enough to be used quite differently from the usual chips or pitches with opened club faces. For instance, when the ball lands on the apron of the green and nestles up against the high fringe, a possible and effective escape route is offered by the bladed wedge. The stroke very much resembles the putting stroke, but is used to best advantage when you can't get a putter between the fringe and the ball. The set up is similar to the address for a putt.

For the bladed wedge, align your feet closed to the target by about an inch to restrict the follow through, and concentrate your weight on the left foot. The ball lies in its usual position just opposite your left heel. Tilt your waist and flex your knees as you would for any other shot. Let your arms hang down naturally with the elbows close to the body throughout impact. Wrists and elbows are bent faintly, but don't break your wrists at impact.

THE RIGHT-HANDED SHOT

The right-handed shot may be an excellent escape from the rough when you cannot take a normal stance. RIGHT: *Stand with your back to your target in a narrow and upright position. The ball is placed in line with your feet, an inch opposite the right foot, and about shoulder-width away from it.* CENTER RIGHT: *The swing is straight back and straight through, but requires a lot of practice because the leading edge cannot be entirely squared to the ball at impact.* FAR RIGHT: *Checking the result.*

THE THREE-
WOOD CHIP

*If you are right up against
the fringe, the three-wood -
with its longer shaft, larger
head and more loft than a
putter - is the ideal club for
the bladed wedge shot.
OPPOSITE, RIGHT: You
treat the bladed wedge like a
long putt. The set up position
is narrow, your stand tall,
and the three-wood gripped
down the shaft. BELOW
RIGHT: Use your putting
stroke and contact the ball in
the middle of the club face as
the thick-soled three-wood
presses down the grass. This
will allow the ball to roll like
a putt. FAR RIGHT: The
follow through again
resembles that of the putting
stroke and determines the
length of the shot.*

Position your hands in line with the ball and aim the bladed sand wedge right at the equator of the ball. When you now release the wedge through the ball at impact, it will appear as if you topped the ball, resulting in more overspin because of the angle at which the ball leaves the clubhead.

You don't have to strike the ball as hard as you would have to with a putter, because the heavy club and broad flange of the sand wedge will cause the ball to roll a little faster than after a putting stroke. Remember to keep your follow through just as long and as high as your backswing so that you don't hit the ball right across the green and out through the back door.

The Three-Wood Chip

A similar putting stroke at the equator of the ball from an equally unpalatable position in the high fringe of the green can be attempted with the three-wood. You will note my particularly narrow and tall stance in the illustrations. The ball is placed as usual opposite my left heel, and although I do not tilt my waist or bend my knees as much as I do to putt, I choke down on the shaft of the three-wood to gain better control for this delicate little shot.

The three-wood chip does not propel the ball as fast as the heavy bladed sand wedge does. This is why you will see a distinct follow through on this shot in the photographs on the following page. The through swing resembles the putting stroke and determines the length of the shot. However, the wood has the added advantage of pushing the high grass down with its large head when it is placed behind the ball.

The higher loft of the three-wood, compared to the putter, barely gets the ball in the air to clear the grass in front of the ball and allows it to run to the hole, just as a putt would.

177

4. Strategy

THE COURSE MANAGEMENT

Many golfers approach the course in such a haphazard way as to make me wonder how they manage their life. Emotions are flying high, tremendous risks are taken without a second thought, tantrums are thrown, and no rational strategy seems to guide their actions. If just some of the sensible principles that keep players out of trouble in their day-to-day affairs were applied to their golf game, their handicaps would drop drastically.

When I play golf, I treat every single stroke – during a tournament as much as during a friendly game – as if my life depended on it. When I go hunting or fishing, I'd like to think that I am better at it than anybody else, because I approach everything I do in life as uncompromisingly as I play golf. Your performance on the golf course will improve dramatically if you treat every minute detail of your game with the same seriousness.

The basis of any game plan involves setting goals. Take care, however, not to confuse wishes and goals. Everybody wishes to play better, but only working at firm goals that are realistic and concrete will make this happen.

You have to list step by step which new shot you want to learn, which club you want to handle better, and which handicap you want to achieve in the long term to get closer to your vision. It doesn't matter if your plans are high-flying. I have very high goals myself. I want to be able to hit each and every golf shot anyone can think of and win each and every tournament I play in.

The Plan for the Round

The overall strategy for playing 18 holes or any part thereof consists of an intimate knowledge of the course you are playing, the weather conditions and prevailing wind directions you are confronted with, the types of grasses on fairways and greens, the type of sand in the bunker and the type of rough with which you have to contend. In other words, you need a yardage meter, a good caddie and the exact geographical dimensions of every trap and every hazard on and around the fairway.

Most of all, a sound strategy requires an intimate knowledge of your playing abilities; the exact distance you can hit each club, the shots you can perform, and, most importantly, the ones you cannot. You need to know your capabilities and stay within your scope. Don't try to hit a shot on a golf course that you haven't practiced. It will only get you into trouble. I won't ever hit a shot with nothing more than the hope of achieving my goal. I need to know that I can do it.

I know exactly how far I can hit every shot, within a yard or two. As an experienced player, you should be able to tell the length of your shots within five yards at least. You must acquire this information not only for your regular shots, but also for your draws and fades. You have to find out what roll each shot generates, and how the angles of your stance and the club face reduce the carry and increase the curve. You must ascertain what length of backswing produces what distance on the fairway, using all of your wedges. It is equally essential to know at what height each of the balls will travel so that you don't end up in the trees you wanted to avoid. You must know the length of shots you can generate in fairway bunkers and in the rough.

You should also take into consideration your form of the day before making your plan. We all have our ups and downs. Don't count on super shots if your more recent rounds were disappointing. Again, you need to plan to play within your limits. I believe it was the great Walter Hagen who said he expected to make at least seven mistakes a round. Take your handicap and add it to Hagen's seven mistakes, and whenever you mishit a shot, just write it off as one of the mistakes allotted to you on any one round. You will then be able to play the round to the best of your abilities that day without letting a duffed shot undermine your confidence.

Don't count on more than two perfect hits per round. That is as many as any player on the PGA Tour can expect. Schedule yourself to play at only 80 percent of your capacity. This will prevent false hopes and frustration over bungled holes. As you lay down the strategy for each of the holes, use your handicap to decide how many strokes you may take to reach the green. Don't base your plan on making par on holes you usually find difficult.

Don't try to outplay your opponents on every shot; you will only end up breathless and out of sorts very soon. Stick to your game plan, regardless of their score. Play within your abilities and budget your energy. You will need extra resources on the final holes of the back nine when you may want to reconsider your strategy if your opponents have got the better of you. You must stick to your game plan until the fifteenth or sixteenth hole at least, but then it may be the time for a gamble.

You want to be well prepared before you tee off. Pack your sweater and your wet weather clothing, and if you play in a cold climate, bring a hand warmer for yourself and your ball. In cold weather, you will lose distance on your shots – more so if your ball is cold, too.

Calculate the climatic conditions into your game plan. Your shots will fly further in higher altitudes, in warm temperatures, and in dry weather. And if you travel, don't forget that flag sticks in the US are seven feet long, but only five in Britain. You may easily misjudge your approach shot if you don't keep this difference in mind. And don't forget to check the local rules.

Have a look around you. How does the overall terrain surrounding the course strike you? Will you have to cope with ridges and ravines in the mountains? Is the ground arid, sporting awe-inspiring cacti-studded wasteland areas? Are you bound to encounter strong winds, as on Scottish links or flat prairie courses? Or will the ball be gobbled up by swamplands if you miss the fairway? The overall view will tell you much about water hazards in the area and warn you of meandering brooks which may cut through the course. You will also get a good idea about the vegetation you will find in the rough, and the number and height of the trees you may have to deal with.

What do you know about the course designer? Is he notorious for blind, narrow holes? Does he have a preference for devious mounds around the green, hiding many yards of ordinary turf behind them? Does he like to create artificial undulations on the fairway, making it difficult to gauge where a ball might roll even after a perfect shot? Does he gravitate towards pot bunkers and difficult trap walls? Is he known for convex greens? Designers tend to build their own rhythm into their courses - and to jolt you out of the routine just when you have picked up the pace. It pays to get to know the characteristics of as many designers as you possibly can.

On the first tee, check the grass. Here is a thumbnail sketch on the playing characteristics of the most frequently used grass types on golf courses: Fescue grass is frequently found on links courses in Britain and other seaside fairways in temperate climates. It has coarse leaves and is usually cut low, producing tight lies on fairways, and you stand to lose distance on it. In the rough, Fescue sports wiry and twirly stems, which entangle clubheads and make escape shots very difficult.

Bentgrass, which is planted liberally in cold to moderate climates in North America, Europe and Japan, features fine blades and tight lies. Your ball will not travel as far as you may wish on the fairways, and you will need a wedge to hit out of high Bentgrass rough.

Bermudagrass is grown with preference in tropical climates in the US, Australia, the Caribbean and Southeast Asia. Depending on the hybrid used, it can be broad- or fine-bladed. On the fairway, the ball will sit up beautifully, and you will hit a good distance, but in the rough, it is stiff and unwieldy and will meddle with your clubhead. Bluegrass and Ryegrass, which is often encountered in cool climates, react in much the same way.

Zoysia is a warm climate grass with coarse leaves, letting your ball sit up well on the holes but turning into a nuisance off the fairways. Poa Annua, a broad-leafed grass found on many courses in Australia, thrives in moist climates and tends to grow fast and in a patchy manner. You may be in for surprises even when it is cut regularly.

The Plan for The Hole

The shrubs, trees, river banks and tall grasses along the borders of the fairway will give you a very good indication of the overall layout of the hole, its shape and width, and the gradation of the terrain. Have a good look at the fairway in front of you. Is it tilted, bowl-shaped, slanting, undulating, bisected? Does it rise or fall, cross a ridge, border a lake? Which way is your ball bound to roll, and for how long? Will a hump, ridge, mound, or slope stop your drive or guide it gently nearer the green? Do the mounds help you to take your bearings or are they deceptive?

Can you cut the corner on a dog-leg? What is the fastest way to the green on a double dog-leg – over, around, under or short of the trees? Your best bet is always to work your strategy from the pin backwards. Mind you, I said the pin, not the green. There is always one ideal angle of attack which will get you there safely and close.

Try to find this approach and see how you can get to that angle from the tee, using a shot you are capable of. Once you have decided on the strategy, stick to it. Courses frequently offer alternative routes to the green - split fairways, for instance - to unsettle you. Don't let the design confuse you.

How dangerous is the rough? Is it so full of tall grass that an escape appears unlikely, provided you find your ball in the first place? Has it been cut, and if so, in what direction? Rough is usually only clipped in one direction, so the ball will either roll further, if it is mown towards the green, or else stop early.

Can you safely aim at the hazards, or are they in contention? Will they save you strokes or will they penalize you? The scorecard should indicate the position and shape of the sand traps and water hazards. When in doubt, the vegetation may serve as marker as well.

Most designers keep some rough between the edge of the fairway and the water which may stop your ball. You may even be able to hit out of shallow water. If you do, beware; water will effectively deloft your club face and result in a flyer. And stay away from the out-of-bounds.

Let your handicap guide you. You don't have to be on the green in regulation. Your goal should be to lose as few strokes as possible. So, whenever you land in trouble, get out of there with your next stroke. Don't try to hit a brilliant shot out of knee-deep rough, unless you are near the end of a round which you are losing. Then take a well-calculated risk; it may well be worth it, and you have nothing to lose.

The Play under Pressure

You hit your stroke more aggressively when the adrenalin is flowing; when your competitors are one up on you; when there are only three more holes to go; when you face that twelve-foot putt to clinch the trophy or fall back into oblivion. You hit longer; you swing faster; and you stand to lose your cool - and your rhythm along with it.

In a tense situation, slow down everything you do. Walk slower, do your pre-shot routine more slowly, and take your time when you select your club. Only if you consciously slow down will you be able to maintain your tempo. Remember Jack Nicklaus; if you want to hit far, take the club away very slowly.

Golf is a game of misses. A scratch player can only hope for one or two perfect shots in a round - no more. Consequently, the final result of the competition depends much less on your good shots than you would expect. Your score stands to suffer more from your bad strokes than a few good hits can offset. Even the great Walter Hagen allowed himself seven mistakes per round. You can easily grant yourself a couple more; just make sure that your mistakes don't cost you more than one stroke each.

Don't try to outplay your competitors. This will only lead to more mistakes. Concentrate on the shot you are about to play. That is all that matters at the moment. Select your clubs carefully. Play one shot at a time. Don't fret about the last hole, don't think about celebrating your victory, and don't worry about your opponent's score. You will then be able to control the damage your mistakes do to your score.

I always play as if I am one shot behind. I thrive on a good challenge and I play aggressively. But while I am constantly looking for a way to cut my score, I assess the situation, and I choose a shot I have practiced before. I take only well-calculated risks because I stay within my limits. The knowledge of your capabilities makes the difference between competitiveness and madness.

THE LIE

After planning the strategy for your round and your hole, you need to decide the angle of attack for every single shot you play. You will be guided by the distance you need to cover, and by the hazards and obstacles in your intended line of flight. However, in the end, the lie of the ball will determine what kind of shot you can or cannot play.

Have a close look at the situation in which you find your ball. Is it in a divot, in a tight lie, on a slope? Will the lie prompt you to hit a fade, a balloon, or a flier? Very often, you will have more than one option to get to your target. The lie may decide for you which one you must choose.

You need to analyze exactly the situation. In which way does the terrain slope - up, down, sideways? How does the ball position affect your trajectory? As a rule of thumb, a downhill lie produces a low trajectory, a long carry and a left-to-right curvature on your trajectory.

An uphill lie creates a high, short flight with a right-to-left deviation. The ball above the feet causes a flat swing and a drawspin, while the ball below the feet results in a steep swing arc and a fade.

The choice of your club depends largely on the distance between your ball and the green. However, since all sloping lies require considerable changes to your stance and swing, you are well advised to stick to short and mid irons when confronted with a severe incline. Long irons are difficult enough to hit straight from a level surface; it is next to impossible to swing fairway woods up and down a slope because of their thick soles.

Once you have decided on the type of shot you want to play, stick to it. The minute you start having second thoughts, you undermine your self confidence. Doubt creeps into your mind, and you begin to think, "Should I have taken the seven iron instead?". Your mind wavers, and your body will waver along with it. Your performance will be a testimony of half-heartedness. You need to evaluate all the information available before you decide on the shot - not after. Then, don't change your decision.

The Ball above the Feet

On Tuesday, during the practice round for the British Open 1993 at Royal St. George's, I wasn't playing very well. My swing was too upright, and I found I had reverted to making mistakes from which I thought Butch had cured me some time ago. So, after the round Butch and I went in search of a hill to practice a flat swing plane by playing with the ball above my feet. After two hours of practice, my swing was back to normal, and I went on to win the tournament with a record score.

The sidehill lie with the ball above your feet naturally flattens out your swing plane. The ball position actually teaches you how to swing around your body. You can't swing in any other way because of both the slope in front of you and the ball position, which is higher than your feet.

The leading edge of the clubhead can never be squared on this sidehill lie, and the club face will close as soon as its heel touches the slope. If you are a right-handed golfer, you will put a drawspin on the ball from this type of lie. A left-handed golfer will fade the ball. Before you set up, you must aim to the right to make an allowance for the curvature in the trajectory.

To hit the ball best from this sidehill lie, take a wide stance. Lean your weight into the slope to maintain a good balance throughout your swing. Choke down on the club, since the slope has in effect moved the ball closer to the clubhead. If you don't grip down on the shaft, you will hit behind the ball, and lose distance - at the very least. Make a wide, shallow arc - which you need to complete - both on the backswing and on the follow through.

The Ball below the Feet

The sidehill lie with the ball below your feet is one of the most difficult swings in golf because gravity tends to pull you down that slope. To offset the fact that your feet are on a higher level than the ball, you must widen your stance to provide a better foundation of your swing. You should get into an almost squatting position, with the knees flexed, to lower your center of gravity. Your weight must be concentrated in your heels to anchor you firmly in this precarious position.

The leading edge of the club cannot be squared to the target at impact with the ball below your feet since the toe of the clubhead may - depending on the incline, the swing plane and the height of the player - hit the ground first. This will, in effect, open your club face and send your ball curving from left to right.

You need to aim left of your target to offset this effect. Be careful not to over-swing from this position. When in doubt, you are better off with a longer club and an easier swing.

THE BALL ABOVE THE FEET

When the ball is above your feet, your swing is restricted by the slope in front of you, which forces you to create a flat swing plane. ABOVE: You must take a wider stance and lean your weight into the slope to maintain your balance. ABOVE RIGHT AND FAR RIGHT: Notice the flat takeaway and backswing, with a full shoulder turn. RIGHT: The leading edge of the club face cannot be squared entirely at impact because of the slope. Control the club face carefully through impact. OPPOSITE: Balance your swing through your knee flex and complete the follow through. The ball will draw.

188

When the ball is below your feet, you need to widen your stance to lower your center of gravity, giving your swing a solid foundation.
OPPOSITE, RIGHT AND FAR RIGHT: *Your knees must be flexed and your waist tilted to reach the ball with your clubhead without having to stretch your arms. Your weight should be concentrated back in your heels.* BELOW RIGHT AND BELOW FAR RIGHT: *As you swing the club, use your knees to prevent gravity from pulling you down the slope towards the ball. The ball will tend to fade from this type of lie.*

The Uphill Lie

The key to hitting off any sloping lie is the alignment of your shoulders. Tilt them parallel to the inclination of the slope so that the vertical axis of your swing is perpendicular to the slope. If you fail to tilt your shoulders properly so that you can swing up the slope, you will end up hitting the hill instead of the ball. Your weight should remain concentrated on your right foot on the uphill lie, and you have to lean into the hill with it to keep your balance.

The swing axis has now in effect moved the ball up in the swing arc so that the clubhead meets the ball high on the upswing. This position lofts the club face and lets the ball balloon. As a consequence, you should take a seven-iron where you would normally take an eight.

When you set up for this shot, you need to make allowances for the fact that an uphill lie causes a right-to-left deviation. Adjust your alignment accordingly. Leave the ball in its regular position, taking a fairly wide, comfortable stance. Align your shoulders to the inclination, and let your well-flexed knees buffer your swing. Take the club away along the slope as far as you can. Make a complete shoulder turn until the club reaches almost parallel to the slope at the backswing. The idea is to swing up the slope.

The Downhill Lie

On the downhill lie, you need to keep your weight back on your left foot to fight gravity's pull down the hill. Adjust your posture until you stand with your legs fairly wide apart so that you are well balanced to make a nice, easy swing. Open your stance to the left of the target because the downhill slope will produce a left-to-right curvature in your trajectory.

Place the ball in the center of your stance so that you don't hit the hill before your clubhead can get to the ball. Align your shoulders parallel to the incline and let your swing follow the slope downwards.

Don't try to pick the ball off the slope, and don't stay level or else you will hit the hill behind the ball. You must have the feeling that you are staying back a little on your right leg as you come through. Again, work with your knees into and through the shot so that you can stay down through the ball.

The ball leaves the club face at a very shallow angle because of the altered swing axis, causing the clubhead to hit the ball on the downswing before it reaches the bottom of the swing arc. The club face is in effect delofted, creating a long carry. So, if you are facing a six-iron shot, take a seven-iron instead.

190

THE ROUGH

OPPOSITE, RIGHT: *On the
uphill lie, you must put your
body on the same angle as
the slope. Lean into the hill
with your weight.* CENTER
RIGHT: *The vertical swing
axis is perpendicular to the
slope, with your weight
concentrated on the right
foot.* FAR RIGHT: *During
your swing, you must work
your knees to balance you
against the slope.* BELOW
RIGHT AND BELOW
CENTER RIGHT: *You need
an early hand release as for
the high ball, to get the ball
up and over the slope.*
BELOW FAR RIGHT: *Keep
your weight balanced
against the slope on the
through swing. Because the
ball will fly higher, you
should take one more club
than you normally would. If
you normally hit a six-iron
for this distance, use a five-
iron.*

The Chinese say that a crisis is a combination of danger and chance. Remember that when your ball next lands in trouble. That difficult ball you find under a tree, at the edge of the water, or in knee-deep grass will give you the chance to use your skill, your knowledge, and your imagination to master a critical situation and emerge victorious.

I believe that confidence is your biggest asset whenever your ball misses the fairway. Incredible opportunities are wasted on golf courses all over the world by professionals and amateurs whose reliance on their performance is shattered by a single ball squirting off into the woodworks. It's obviously no use to remember the shot you pulled out-of-bounds on this very hole only last week, or the stroke you lost on the last hole, when your ball found the water. If you have confidence in your own abilities, you won't lose your cool under pressure.

When you encounter trouble, you first have to assess the situation. What are the possibilities for an escape? Which is the biggest problem under the circumstances? Which of your shot techniques can take care of the situation best? What is the safest manner to tackle the problem? What is the riskiest? Is there any other way out, which you have not thought of before and which may save you a stroke? Improvise. Let your experience guide you. Also consider your opponents. How did they fare so far? Is it time for a gamble?

Whenever you are playing your shots from bad lies, from underneath the tree or from under a branch, you have to use your skill for playing low and high balls, fades and draws, depending on the situation.

The Cut-Up Wood from Light Rough

Playing a fairway wood out of the rough requires either a rather good lie - such as low grass - or a very lofted wood - such as a six-, seven- or even a nine-wood. Since most advanced golfers carry only a four-wood or a five-wood in their bags, the irons are their only possible tool to escape from troublesome rough. However, if the ball sits in grass of no more than one or two inches in height, you may take your highest lofted wood and cut the ball.

Set up for a fade by opening your stance, aiming to the left of the target with the ball back in the center of your stance. This will allow you to swing at a steeper plane and hit the ball more directly, without getting too much grass between the clubhead and the ball. Open your club face to offset the effect of

192

On the downhill lie, you can use one club less because the ball tends to fly lower and longer. RIGHT AND FAR RIGHT: *The downhill lie requires a wider stance to build a good foundation for your swing. The swing must follow the slope downwards. Do not try to pick the ball off the ground, as you will hit on top of the ball.* OPPOSITE, RIGHT: *Even on top of the backswing, most of the weight remains on the left foot.* BELOW RIGHT: *In spite of the restricted weight transfer, the head stays behind the ball.* OPPOSITE, BELOW RIGHT: *Work with your knees into and through this shot so that you can stay down through the ball.*

194

OPPOSITE, RIGHT: *To hit the ball off a hardpan lie you must stand taller to pick the ball up clean. Notice my narrow stance, the lack of flex in my knees and the tilt in my waist.* CENTER RIGHT: *Use your regular backswing.* BELOW RIGHT: *Do not use as much leg drive through the impact zone on this shot to prevent the clubhead from bouncing off the surface and topping the ball.* BOTTOM FAR RIGHT: *You want to keep a firm left wrist at impact, and swing through the shot.* FAR RIGHT: *The hands are in line with the ball at address.* BELOW FAR RIGHT: *The right hand leads through impact.*

the grass which tends to close the club face. Pick the club up a little steeper on the backswing so that you can hit down on it through impact.

Distinctly draw the club back to the outside, deviating from your normal swing path parallel to the target line, immediately on the takeaway. Stay on the outside-in path throughout your entire swing. At impact, the clubhead will hit the ball on the downswing with a descending blow and an open club face, causing the ball to veer off to the left at a very steep angle initially. The flight pattern will revert to a true fade further down. In spite of the descending blow, you will not impart much backspin on the ball because some grass will invariably get in front of the club face at impact.

The Tall Grass

Tall grass will wrap around the club when you swing down and close the club face. If your ball is sitting down in such rough, you have to choose a club with more loft. A straight-faced club won't get the ball out of tall grass at all.

Move the ball back in your stance so that your club face catches it at the bottom of the swing arc. Open the club face at address. On the takeaway, cock the club up steeply to set up for an abrupt swing plane. Beat down on the ball and make it jump out of that grass. Due to the open club face, you will produce a slight fade, so make allowances for the sidespin when you aim.

The Hardpan Lie

From a hardpan lie, you have to pick the ball cleanly off the surface. To do so, stand a little taller to the ball, with your feet close together. Keep your wrists stiff throughout the swing, to creating a shallower swing angle so that you can sweep the ball off the hardpan lie better.

There is not much leg drive through the impact zone on this shot, preventing the clubhead from bouncing off the surface and topping the ball. Keep a firm left wrist, and let your right hand lead through impact. You don't want to try to hit it hard or beat down on the ball.

As you can see in the pictures, I did not use a lot of wristcock on the backswing when I attacked the pin some 110 yards further down from a concrete-like hardpan lie. I took a pitching wedge, hit it with an easy three-quarter swing, and picked the ball off beautifully.

196

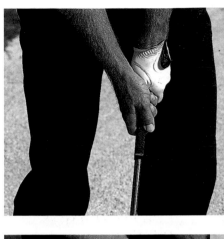

The Powdery Lie

Pine needles may not be the prototype for a powdery lie, but they require the same kind of shot since they cushion the ball in the same way as fine sand would. You cannot ground your club because the ball is likely to move. So, at address, let the clubhead hover behind the ball.

Address the powdery lie like you would your regular chip, using a nine-iron or a pitching wedge. The narrow stance and the ball position remain identical, but you need to stand a little taller. You don't use much weight transfer or leg action, due to the rather short swing. Keep your weight on the left foot and your hands well in front of the ball, in line with your left thigh.

Place the ball back in your stance by about two inches and make your usual pendulum-like chip movement. During the backswing and follow through, the wrists barely bend and remain straight through impact. The clubhead stays low during takeaway and through swing. Keep the wrists passive, with the back of the left hand actually leading the clubhead through impact. Don't allow the left hand to break down. Since the forward hand position has, in effect, neutralized some of the loft of the club, the result of the chip is a short, low flight of the ball and a long roll.

The Covered Lie

A ball buried in pine needles so that you can hardly see it demands an explosion shot much like the one in a bunker. Set up with your left foot, knee and hip open to the left of the target, and an open sand wedge. Focus on a spot in the pine needles two or three inches behind the ball, which lies in its usual position opposite your left heel.

Start to cock your wrist very early in the backswing, creating a steep angle in the takeaway. Rotate your shoulders just a little, depending on the length of the backswing and the intended carry of your ball. The steep swing arc allows your right hand to slap the wedge into the needles with the right hand about two to three inches behind the ball through impact. The sole of the wedge will throw pine needles and the ball out of the rough. The speed of the clubhead through impact and the length of the follow through determine the distance the ball will travel.

THE
POWDERY
LIE

ABOVE: *Pine needles may not be the prototype for a powdery lie, but they require the same kind of shot since they cushion the ball in the same way as fine sand would.* OPPOSITE, FAR LEFT: *Off of this type of lie, you do not want to ground the club because the ball may move.* LEFT: *While you will use your normal chipping motion for this shot, you also need to pick the ball off the top of the pine needles.* BELOW FAR LEFT: *Keep your weight on your left side and stand tall. Try not to use as much leg action on this shot.* BELOW LEFT: *The pine needles splash away from the clubhead at impact, even though the ball was hit clean.*

THE COVERED LIE

ABOVE: *A ball buried in pine needles as no bunker could bury them.* ABOVE RIGHT: *You must treat this shot like a bunker shot and address it with an open stance and an open club face.* ABOVE FAR RIGHT: *You have to hit behind the ball just like an explosion shot in the bunker. Cock your wrists and the clubhead at a steep angle on the backswing.* RIGHT: *You have to hit the pine needles with your right hand on the downswing.* OPPOSITE: *The follow through determines the length of the flight.*

THE WEATHER

Sunshine, wind and rain on the day of your round can lead your game to new heights or ruin your scores. In cold weather, your drives carry little and roll less. In warm, dry weather, your chips bounce and run past the flagsticks and through the greens. Dew, rain and sprinkler drops let your putts crawl at a snail's pace before running out of breath two feet short of the cup.

Humidity in the air flattens the trajectory of your ball and stops your long game short. Soggy soil turns you into an expert on local winter rules, ruins your best pair of pants, and dirties your hands every time you fumble a plugged ball out of the mud. I hear there are golf courses in Iceland where snow is treated as casual water... Then again, there are courses in Australia where sand is treated as permanent green.

Little can be done about the climate of a place - except for studying the local rules, packing the woollies and the umbrella, stocking the hand warmer and the water-resistant jacket, and buying sunscreen and mosquito-repellent. It helps to bear a couple of general guidelines in mind.

As an experienced golfer, you also have tried and tested for yourself that whenever you hit downhill, you gain about 10 yards - or one club's difference - on your shots. Now, if you play on very dry soil, do you gain another 10 yards on your shots? In principle, the answer is yes; in practice, the distance you actually gain from dry soil and dry weather may be much more than that, or much less.

You have to consider the trajectory of your shot to make an educated guess about the yardage you gain. The steeper the line of flight - its height versus its length - the less roll you will get on normal turf, and the fewer jumps and bounces you will see on very dry grass. In other words, if you play the approach with an eight-iron on level, normal ground, and a nine-iron on a downhill slope under the same conditions, you should play it with your pitching wedge on very dry turf. That is, if it is not newly watered or still enveloped in morning dew, (in which case, revert to your nine-iron).

Now, if this said dry hole course happens to lie in a desert 5,000 feet above sea level, and if the sun burns down on you at over 100 degrees Fahrenheit, your ball travels further still. If you don't have a gap wedge, make a three-quarter swing with your pitching wedge, but don't use your sand wedge. It will only bounce off the dry soil.

Remember however, that only the heat, the dry and thin air, and the slope give you extra carry. The dry soil merely gives you extra roll, which may be a nuisance if the green is tiny, and if the pin sits next to a bunker or on the far side of a pond. You can only add up your yardage gains if you have an open green to play with.

Let's assume you are playing the very same hole again a year later. It's May, the sun laughs down on you, and it hasn't rained in ages, but the designer has since lengthened the hole in preparation for a major tournament. The green has been moved 50 yards further afield. What used to be an easy nine-iron shot now looks like it takes all of a four-iron, although it is still a downhill shot.

Should you now — in warm, thin air and on dry ground — use your five-iron? Yes, provided that the new green is level with the old green. Why? The four-iron comes naturally with a long roll because it lands on the grass at a very shallow angle. The dryer the ground, the further the ball skates. Where you gained ten yards on the nine-iron shot, you may gain 15 or 20 yards with a four-iron. You just have to be very sure about the carry of your shot and the landing and rolling areas available.

You will have to keep all possible variables in mind when you consider the weather factors. There are so many variations to consider: one grass doesn't react like the other; one type of soil is harder than the other; and the wind may offset any or all of the advantages gained. In the end you will have to experiment a lot.

If we look back at our downhill hole, for instance, and consider the implications if the green had been moved 50 yards but further downhill than the former green was situated on a very steep gradient, you can probably use a six-iron instead of the five-iron. However, if the green was repositioned slightly up on the opposite ridge, presenting you with a downhill shot but an uphill roll, you probably would still need your four-iron.

When the wind is in play, the situation changes dramatically. You have to assess, if you are dealing with a shot into the wind, downwind, into a right-to-left or a left-to-right crosswind or into a wind blowing from a different angle. You can then either use the wind to your advantage by working your shots into or around it, or you can ride the wind by simply adjusting your alignment to offset its effect.

A tailwind largely undoes the effects of backspin and sidespin on a ball. Your fades and your draws will fly straighter than you intended. The distance of a low-flying ball will be shortened severely by a tailwind, because it knocks the ball to the ground quickly, but the carry of your high shots increases drastically.

THE THREE-IRON WITH THE WIND

The three-iron shot with the wind is set up like a high shot. RIGHT: *You need to place the ball an inch forward from your normal long iron address position. The head has thus moved behind the ball to allow for an early release.* FAR RIGHT: *The takeaway is as wide as for the normal three-iron shot.* BELOW RIGHT: *The club has almost reached parallel to the ground at the top of the backswing and the shoulder turn is complete.* BELOW FAR RIGHT: *The follow through is the same as for the regular swing, however, the ball will fly higher initially and then be carried by the wind further than your regular distance.*

The seven-iron shot against the wind follows the set-up for a low, boring shot. FAR LEFT: *The ball has moved back in the stance for a low trajectory.* LEFT: *The takeaway clearly shows the wide, flattened swing arc I use for a low trajectory shot.* BELOW FAR LEFT: *The backswing is shortened to almost three-quarter's.* BELOW LEFT: *The follow through is wide, but short. The ball will bore into the wind.*

You can gain genuine airborne distance in a tailwind, while its effect on the ground is negligible. Take one club less, but bear in mind that tailwinds also reduce the height of the flight on your short game. Tee up.

A headwind emphasizes the backspin and the sidespin on your ball, and causes your fades and draws to curve more. The straight shots tend to balloon and are much reduced in length. You are well advised to take a four-iron instead of a five-iron, and keep the ball very low. Tee down.

The Play in the Crosswind

A crosswind exaggerates both the backspin and the sidespin that curves with it, while straightening the curvature of a ball that flies into it. It will also shorten the trajectory of a fade or draw that comes head-on. As a rule of thumb, you gain more distance off the tee if you ride the wind. So if you are facing a right-to-left crosswind, set up aiming to the right of the target in proportion to the strength of the wind, and let the wind carry the ball to the target.

Iron shots, however, lend themselves to be worked into the crosswind to your advantage. When you encounter a right-to-left crosswind, for example, hit a fade into the wind, back to the right using the wind as a bumper. Depending on the force of the gale and the curvature in your trajectory, your fade will initially fly further to the left and curve back to the right less than it normally would. Since the trajectory of your shot will be shortened, take one club more than you need.

The Three-Iron with the Wind

To utilize a tailwind to your advantage, you need a high trajectory. If you just make your regular swing, the wind will knock your ball to the ground quickly. Take an iron, rather than a wood, with the wind and play it like a high shot. It is very difficult to swing a wood properly in strong gales, because its long shaft and thick clubhead offer too much resistance to the wind. It is also not easy to get the ball airborne with a wood before the wind blows the ball down.

During the 1994 British Open Championship at Turnberry, the gales were so strong that I had to lean with my body weight against them just to stay balanced, and my three-wood stayed in the bag during most of the tournament. So, if you play in turbulent weather, use your three-iron for your longer shots as I did in the photographs on page 204.

To set up for a shot with a tailwind, place the ball about an inch up in your stance, opposite the ball of your left foot. Your head now moves behind the ball, allowing it to stay back as you swing through long enough to square the club face through impact. The head position also causes an early release of the hands, allowing you to throw the ball up in the air better.

Take the club away slowly to set up for as wide a backswing as you usually make with your three-iron. Complete your normal shoulder turn, so that you can sweep the ball away on the downswing. Let the centrifugal force carry your hands and shoulders around until your follow through is complete. The ball will balloon initially, until the wind gets hold of it and carries it further than your regular three-iron distance.

It is essential that you don't allow the wind to wreck havoc with your timing. Wind tends to tempt golfers into swinging extra hard or fast. Observe your pre-shot routine, then, slow down and swing easy.

The Seven-Iron against the Wind

Crosswinds and headwinds exaggerate both sidespin and backspin. If you put too much backspin on the ball, it will shoot up into the air, and the wind will carry it higher still. To control your ball into the wind better, you have to hit it down lower with a shallow swing plane and a three-quarter arc.

Headwinds tempt many golfers to hit extra hard to offset the loss of distance they suffer from it. Let me guard against this attempt. The harder you hit the ball, the more backspin you put on the ball. This, in turn, sends the ball skywards, and you'll lose even more distance. It is important for you to take a longer club and swing easy so that you can control your golf swing.

In the photographs on page 205, I use a seven-iron against the wind, with a flatter, lower swing to bore the ball through the turbulence. The shot can be played equally well with a longer iron, although these tend to be more difficult to handle in strong winds.

At address, move the ball an inch back in the stance from its usual position opposite the left heel to trim the backspin. As you will remember, the less backspin is imparted on the ball, the flatter the flight.

Keep your feet wider apart than you normally would to lower the center of gravity. Set up for your flat, shallow swing plane by initiating a wide, low takeaway, which is mirrored exactly on the wide but short through swing. Restrict your backswing to a three-quarter's arc to control the club face

207

through the ball better. The shallow downswing into the ball imparts power and speed to the ball without making it soar.

The Play in the Rain

Playing in the rain - particularly in cold, strong winds - is not only uncomfortable, it is also frustrating. The ball just doesn't seem to move. Take a three-iron instead of a five-iron, as you stand to lose both carry and roll in the rain. Pick the ball crisply off the fairway, since the wet soil is heavy and will stick to your clubhead. If it just started raining on a very dry soil, you'll only lose carry, and can take out the four-iron.

Try to keep your body warm by wearing several layers of clothes. You need to feel that you are still able to make your swing, and not that you have become as bulky as an ice bear. Use a hand warmer or large, insulated gloves between the shots to be able to feel the club. Most of all, try to keep yourself and the equipment dry. If your clubheads get wet, be prepared for flyers, since water has much the same effect as grass between clubhead and ball.

The Play on Soggy Soil

On soggy soil, you cannot beat down on the ball because the ground is wet underneath it. Leave your fairway woods in your bag since they will only dig into the mud with their thick clubheads.

Stand a little taller and open your stance to set up for a steep swing plane since you need to pick the golf ball from the turf. Open the club face as well to send the ball off on a straight line. Don't forget to flex your knees so that you won't slip on the treacherous ground. For better control, use your three-quarter swing.

By now, you should be well equipped for almost any situation you may encounter on a golf course, provided you have put in enough hours on the range. Enjoy your new shotmaking skills and better scores. Happy golfing!